The
Expert
Author
Effect

TO ELENA

GO FOR IT!

Dr. Paul Newton & Bob Burnham

The Expert Author Effect

ISBN-13: 978-0-9970968-5-9
ISBN-10: 0-9970968-5-3

Published by: Celebrity Expert Author
http://celebrityexpertauthor.com

Canadian Address:
501- 1155 The High Street,
Coquitlam, BC, Canada
V3B.7W4
Phone: (604) 941-3041
Fax: (604) 944-7993

US Address:
1300 Boblett Street
Unit A-218
Blaine, WA 98230
Phone: (866) 492-6623
Fax: (250) 493-6603

Contents

INTRODUCTION

*"When you write and publish an expert book
and use it to grow your business,
you can automate attracting perfect customers
and never have to do sales and marketing again."*

Dr. Paul:

Being in business can be hard—really hard. People who aren't business owners don't understand what it takes for you to keep your doors open doing what you are really good at and love. It may always seem to be the back and forth between feast or famine. When it's good, it's really good, but when you don't have new clients, patients, or customers coming in, it becomes painful really fast.

When we start out in business, we have the passion and fire in us to build something great. We are doing what we love with the hopes of creating a really good life for ourselves. But the constant struggle of having to look for new people to serve can start to wear down that passion really fast. The reality is, every business must focus on sales and marketing, or it cannot stay in business—and most of us did not have big dreams of being a marketer or a salesperson.

Wouldn't it be nice if sales and marketing could be really easy—if you could just leave it on autopilot and know that it is getting done? Sadly, when we don't pay attention and just focus on what we like doing, the clients seem to dwindle and we find ourselves needing to turn our attention back to sales and marketing. If you don't have it handled, it always seems to come back and bite your butt.

But there is good news. There is a way that you can make sales and marketing so simple that you can set it up once and practically forget about it while you focus on what you're passionate about. It's a strategy that few people use, but the few who have been using it for a lot of years will tell you that it's always worked, it's still working, and it will keep on working. That strategy is writing an expert book and using it to attract perfect customers for your business.

We are here to tell you that you can focus on this one simple, elegant strategy and use it to generate all the leads your business will ever need. You will be able to attract perfect customers for any business, whether you're looking for people to buy your products and services, patients for your practice, or clients of any kind for your professional services. When you write and publish an expert book and use it to grow your business, you can automate the attraction of perfect customers and never have to do sales and marketing again.

Let us introduce ourselves. We are a two-man team that makes up Celebrity Expert Author Publishing. I'm Dr. Paul Newton, a chiropractor, and my business partner, Bob Burnham, is a multiple seven-figure entrepreneur and business owner. We have come to love the strategy of writing and publishing an expert book to handle your sales and marketing and grow your business. It's how we help our clients, and it's the only marketing strategy that we use in our business.

Bob:

When I started my carpet cleaning company in the mid-1970's, marketing was straightforward and simple. It really was a simple mathematical equation. But in the last few decades, so many different avenues have become available that marketing becomes complex and difficult, if you buy into them all.

One of the first things that we did when I opened up shop was send out pink flyers. They advertised the living room, dining room, and hall for $39.95. We were getting a 7 to 10 percent return! If you were getting that return on flyers today, you'd be doing the happy dance and driving a Rolls Royce. But that did not last. When we stopped doing flyers, the return was less than a quarter of one percent.

The story gets even funnier here, because we started doing telephone sales. For every one hundred people we called, fifty people would get their carpets cleaned. Half the people we called became customers! Needless to say, we ditched the flyers. But once again, the same thing happened: by the time we stopped cold calling people, we were lucky to get even one or two customers per hundred calls.

I always had to look for different ways to market my business. I read a book by a realtor who was doing so well that he had his own private jet. I thought, "Man, I need to do what this guy is doing!"

He had written a book to position himself as the go-to realtor. This realtor always gave his clients a copy of his book, and he sold a lot of real estate.

I thought, "Jeez, that's a really good idea," but I put it on hold because I was still making lots of money doing telephone sales. It wasn't until decades later, when these marketing strategies weren't working as well anymore, that I started thinking, "What can I do that is still working?"

There are so many marketing methods out there now that it would be crazy to list them all. The one I did try next was, of course, writing and positioning my business with a book. My carpet cleaning business had evolved into a fire and flood restoration company, and I used a book called How to Make a Million Dollars in Your Home Service Business to position me as the expert in the industry.

It worked brilliantly. In fact, I doubled my business that year. Even though I didn't use the expert book strategy to market my business until three decades later, it worked as well, if not better than it did for that realtor! And it is still working for us today.

Dr. Paul:

When I got into business, it was by necessity. In 1997, I graduated from chiropractic college. To start work as a chiropractor, I first had to open a business. I got even more loans than I already had and opened a beautiful office. I was so excited to start helping people, but I was not a business person. I didn't want to do sales. I didn't want to do marketing.

I quickly discovered that just hanging out a shingle didn't work if you wanted to eat or pay back loans. I had to do something to get some new patients in the door.

After dropping thousands of flyers, I got only one new patient. I spent thousands of dollars running ads in the local paper before I realized I was wasting my money. I stood at booths in malls and at shows, which was painful although somewhat effective. This was not the glorified vision that I had had of helping lots of happy patients and living the good life.

I found that the best way to get new patients was by speaking. I would hold workshops in my office, and tell people exactly how I could help them get the results they wanted with their backs, their pain, and their health. I jumped at any opportunity I got to speak to groups or in people's workplaces. People who came to my workshops were better patients and referred lots more of their friends, family, and co-workers.

I knew that when I had an audience, I could get new patients, but I always needed to attract new people. Soon, I became good at using all sorts of methods to promote my workshop series that I held in my office monthly. We used old school methods like putting up posters around town, and new school methods like posting online and via social media. I started a MeetUp group that continually brought people into my office for my workshops every month; that group is still working today. Speaking was the one marketing method that worked well and actually got better over the whole sixteen years I was in practice.

Bob and I met in Phoenix, Arizona, at a friend's seminar. We had been in the same business mastermind but had never met. We started talking about marketing, and really hit it off.

Coming into the business world in different times, we had different experiences with marketing fads as they came and went. We realized that the half-life of marketing strategies seemed to be getting shorter and shorter. New marketing strategies were coming out daily, but their effectiveness was short-lived. In fact, by the time someone was teaching it to you, it wasn't working anymore.

Nowadays, you hear that you need a presence on LinkedIn, Facebook, Twitter, and YouTube as a baseline. But what about Yelp, Instagram, Pinterest, and all the others? The bigger question is, "Is it actually yielding buyers for your business?"

We knew that people do business with the people they know, like, and trust. While everyone else is trying to build a virtual relationship online, we found that the best customers, who spend the most money, stay the longest, and refer are the ones we've connected with through speaking or with our books. "Old school" marketing is the new "new school."

Bob and I really connected on these old school methods of building trust with people, and we started to help each other. The result was a partnership and a book we co-authored called How to Be a Celebrity Expert Author. We showed people how they could use the expert book and speaking strategy to be the leading expert in any field. This book was great for people with an interest in sales and marketing. But most people who are in business just want to do what they love and have the sales and marketing handled. Writing an expert book can give you just that. That's why we wrote this book.

More than likely, you have already been wanting to write a book. Don't worry if you don't know where to start, don't know what to write about, or don't think you're that interesting. We want to show you just how easy it can be to put together an expert book that connects with your perfect customers and draws them into your business. We'll show you the sweet spot for the most effective expert book, and you'll find out how to make the writing process so simple that you could finish it in fewer than sixty days if you wanted to.

Our formula for writing your expert book that automates your sales and marketing is simple. There are five steps:

1. Decide on the goal of your book (get leads, increase referrals, retain clients, close bigger sales, become the leading expert).

2. Create your writing plan and get a credible publisher.

3. Write and publish your book fast so it can automate your sales and marketing.

4. Give your book to potential leads, and let it turn them into perfect customers.

5. Make more money doing what you love, knowing that your sales and marketing are handled.

The fact that most people think writing and publishing a book is hard is a good thing—it just makes those of us who have done it look so much better. Since so few people are using this strategy to grow their business, it just makes you stand out even more.

Even the business owners who have written a book have usually written the wrong book, and it's not doing a thing for their bottom line. But don't worry. By the time you finish reading, you will know how to write the right book and put your sales and marketing on autopilot.

Before we get started, we want to give you our Celebrity Expert Author (CEA) Right Book Template. You can use this to build the framework for your expert book so that you write the right book that does your sales and marketing, and fills your business with perfect customers.

We're also giving you our CEA Storytelling Template so you can start gathering your success stories that will connect with and convert your perfect leads. You can download both of these templates at CelebrityExpertAuthor.com/Templates.

CHAPTER 1:

WHY A BOOK IS BETTER THAN ANY OTHER MARKETING TOOL & ALWAYS WILL BE

"When you write the right book, you can
put in the effort once and then use it for years."
". . . the clients who your book brings invest three times
as much, are loyal three times longer,
and will refer you ten times more."

Bob:

Marketing. You know you need it, but you're a professional, a specialist, an expert. You're trained in your field and you have expertise that can help a lot of people, but you're not a marketer. You know you need marketing, but how do you do it? Who do you turn to for help? It's just like an expensive and slippery fish.

You are the expert in your field. If everybody knew that, they would be flooding your business. But you need clients. How do you get these? You'd love to just hang out a shingle and have the world flock to your door, but unfortunately, that's just not the way it is.

So we start going through the whole process of asking, "How do I get clients? What do I budget for this? Who do I trust to really help me with marketing?"

There are just so many different avenues for marketing your business. That's the slippery fish. It's overwhelming, especially nowadays with the Internet and social networking. Facebook, Twitter, Instagram, Pinterest, LinkedIn, Yelp, YouTube, MeetUp, Google AdWords, banner ads, podcasts, email newsletters, blogging, trade shows and events, networking in general, print ads, radio, TV, direct mail. Where does it end?

Even to just pick out and implement a couple of the strategies from the list I just generated, takes a learning curve, time, and money. We just want to do what we love to do, and that's run our businesses and serve our clients.

Marketing's something we know is really, really important, but we just don't know how to go about it. Who do you trust? Where do you go? Everybody has got this great idea about what's working and what you need, and they're happy to take a lot of money to do it for you. But the fact of the matter is there are probably 20,000 to 30,000 advertising messages bombarding us every day. Marketing is too big an investment of time, energy, and money to just be drowned out by all the noise out there.

The choices we make for our marketing plan really can determine how successful we're going to be in the long run. You certainly don't want to blow your budget on something that was working yesterday but won't be in a few months. That's the big problem with all these approaches and all the marketing noise. Most often, by the time you're hearing about the strategy, it's been on the decline and is not producing half the results that the person telling you about it claims.

You'll have so-called marketing experts out there saying, "You've got to be found everywhere, and if you don't keep up on a constant basis, it won't work. It's the repetition and consistency that gets results with all these avenues for marketing."

My list of marketing channels earlier is not even a comprehensive list. When you pick up one, you end up dropping three others. It's impossible to stay on top of it. But that's exactly where we have found a vein of opportunity that has worked exceptionally well for a long time. And it will continue to work well for a long time.

It's simple, requires little to no effort once you get it going, and it gets great results. This is not like all the other strategies that are bombarding people out there. It makes a huge impression, and because people think it's hard to do (it can be, if you don't know where to start), hardly anyone is using it.

This strategy is positioning and marketing your business with a book. What we mean by that is writing an expert book that you use for marketing your business, not marketing and selling the book.

Writing an expert book with the goal of automating your sales and marketing is something that you only have do once if you do it right. You put in the effort at the front end, and it just continues to work for you, and it pays you back for years to come.

People are receiving about 5,000 ad impressions a day. That means that throughout the course of a single day, they are seeing ads going by on buses, ads on TV, ads on Facebook and on all the different social media channels.

There are all these things grabbing at their attention, and people are numb. They are looking for opportunities to get rid of these advertisements. Nobody wants to see them. They are running to the washroom or to the kitchen during TV ads. They're closing all the windows that are flashing at them on the computer and in fact ⅓ of internet users have ad blocker software. They're throwing out junk mail and doing whatever they can to get away from all the marketing. So how do you make sure that you can be seen or heard through all this noise?

On top of it all, the lifespan of all these ads are a flash in the pan. That bus drives by, that thing on Facebook is here one minute and gone the next. Not only are people trying to avoid your marketing message, you might not even have it somewhere that they will see it in the first place.

But with a book, you're definitely standing out in the crowd. When a book ends up in their hands, it's something tangible, new, and interesting. How often does anyone ever give you a book? This marketing tool stays with people for not just that minute or so that a commercial or newspaper ad might be in front of them. This book is going to stay on a desk for months. It may remain on a shelf in their library for years. Your message has legs because nobody ever throws away a book. Nobody ever keeps a brochure library in their home, but they do keep books. It's just a completely different energy from all the other marketing media out there.

I've been to people's houses and seen my book sitting on their table or on their bookshelf. People have it beside their beds, and they think of you every time they see it. It's not perceived as marketing. It's a work of time, effort, and value. All the other brochures, pamphlets, and packages go into the trash, but the book is something that people treat with respect. The best part is, it keeps making them think of you.

When you write the right book, you can put in the effort once and then use it for years. It's the brochure that nobody will ever throw out. It's the business card that you hand to anybody who is a potential client, that keeps working for you for months or years after they get it.

Give it away. Don't sell it, because with the right book, you can actually select the clients you want and repel the people you don't want. You can write your book in such a way that it will tell the right person how you can help them, and tell the people that don't fit the bill that this is the wrong place for them. When you encounter people who are perfect customers for your business, you don't want the risk of them not buying your book. You want that book in their hands, working on them, converting them into lifetime customers for you.

Research actually shows that people who read your book are going to be the best clients. If somebody is looking in a particular area for information or to follow up, one of the things they will do is start reading up on it. So, of course, when they get an expert book, they feel that they are getting the best information on what they're looking for. As the author of that book, you're in a better position than all your competitors. Because you're the only one with a book that is teaching them about exactly what they need, it solidifies in their mind that you are the person to contact.

As the expert and the author of that book, you are the one who is trusted for that information. For that very reason, the people that come into contact with you through your book are going to stay with you three times as long, spend three times as much money, and refer you ten times more often.

The compounding effect is that the clients who comes through your book are obviously worth a lot more than leads that come in through a brochure or other means. Whether it's Google AdWords, a Facebook ad, or any of these other things that we mentioned earlier, in the long run, those are more expensive means of advertising.

When you really understand what a perfect customer is worth to your business, you will see just how valuable it is to invest in a way to get more of them through your door. A book that is written with the express purpose of connecting with the needs of the perfect customer you want in your business is not seen as an advertising.

Even though it might be several thousand dollars to set up once, the long-term return on investment is absolutely spectacular with a book. I've had a book out for ten years now, and I'm still getting clients from that book. People still write to me today and say, "I got your book eight, nine, or ten years ago, and I want your help with my book because you wrote the book on how to write a book."

A book works for marketing both short- and long-term. No other type of advertising will keep working for years or has that return on investment. Writing an expert book is, in fact, the only marketing you'll ever need once you get it done.

The beauty of what we're writing about is that people don't see it as marketing or advertising. You're not looked at as a salesman. You come in under the radar. People welcome you with respect because you're an author, and then they sell themselves.

When you consider the costs of marketing, it's easy to spend thousands of dollars a month on Facebook ads, print ads, direct mail, Google AdWords, or the like. This may bring in unqualified leads at best, but as soon as that ad is gone, it stops working and you must spend more money to get it working again.

However, investing several thousand dollars to produce a book will get you a quality lead who will spend more money, stay longer, and happily refer you or pass on your book. Your book is an unpaid sales force that works for you twenty-four hours a day, seven days a week, three hundred sixty-five days a year. You just can't get better marketing any cheaper.

The Lifetime Value of a Perfect Customer

Consider what a client is actually worth to you. The lifetime value of a client is the amount of money that one client will bring to your business over the time that they remain your client. The way you figure this out is by adding up all the money that that client spends in all the years they stay with you.

On top of that, you must add in all the money that the referrals from that client spend with you in that time frame. This ends up being a very big number, and it makes you value your clients a whole lot more. It also shows that spending money to get quality clients is a solid investment.

One of my first businesses was in carpet cleaning, which wasn't really a big-dollar item. Back in the '70s, my company offered to clean your living room, dining room, and hall for $39.95. That wasn't a lot of money, even back then. This got us in the door, but most clients would spend some extra money on Scotch Guard or extra bedroom cleaning, and the average bill ended up being around $120.00. There are many clients who would have it done twice a year.

So, to calculate the lifetime value of a carpet cleaning client in the '70s, let's say one customer spends $240.00 a year. Many customers will stay with you for a minimum of ten years; $240.00 times ten years is $2,400.00.

What if you've done a really good job for that client? Let's say they give you two referrals per year, or twenty referrals over their lifetime. If you multiply those twenty referrals by $2,400.00 over their lifetime, that's another $48,000.00.

The actual lifetime value of that one client who came in on a $39.95 offer is then $2,400.00 plus $48,000.00, or a whopping $50,400.00! That's a big number, and it doesn't even take into account that many of those referral clients will also refer you.

My family's favorite restaurant chain, Earl's, is so successful because they know the value of their customers. In fact, I had heard that the owner, Buzz, was so big on customer service because his first restaurant chain, Fuller's, did not consider how much a customer was worth. They went under.

You can tell that Earl's knows about the lifetime value of a customer because any time that we had any complaints about the meal—which was very, very seldom, they would ask, "Is there a problem?"

They would replace the dinner for a different meal if we wanted to, at no charge. They knew that not-so-good meal that night might cost them $20.00—a small price to pay to keep my family and me happy. That's how you treat customers who could be worth hundreds of thousands of dollars.

We were sure to always tell our carpet cleaners the value of a customer, because they definitely treated a client worth $50,400.00 better than one worth $39.95. You can always tell the restaurants and carpet cleaners who see you as a $20.00 or $39.95 customer. This is another reason we have written this book. It's such an important point to hit home. We know from our past track record and that of hundreds of our clients that even just one lead from this book will cover our investment more than ten times over.

When you consider that your ideal client's lifetime value can easily be in the hundreds of thousands of dollars, it makes the investment in writing an expert book to attract the perfect customer a no-brainer. Especially when the clients who come through your book invest three times as much, are loyal three times longer, and will refer you ten times more. It's a really beautiful thing that works for almost any business you're in.

Not only has it worked for a long time, it's going to continue to work for a long time. Not very many professionals, business owners, and entrepreneurs do it because they think that it's a lot of work. Because of this fact, the market will never become saturated with this kind of marketing. That's what makes it such a great opportunity for people who are willing to get past the barrier of needing to become an author.

We're here to tell you that it's not a lot of work at all to write a book that positions your business and gets you perfect customers. This book explains exactly what you need to write in your expert book so that it targets your perfect customer and does your sales and marketing for you.

If you follow our CEA Right Book Template and our CEA Storytelling Template, you will have what you need to write your book fast. If you haven't downloaded them yet, go to CelebrityExpertAuthor.com/Templates and get them now.

Just imagine having clients that come to you feeling like they know you. They aren't shopping around and they're not tire-kickers. They see the value in your service. They know exactly how to take advantage of and utilize your products and services, and the benefits of doing so long-term. They want the results that you say you can get, and they're willing to do what it takes. You can create all this and more by following our formula for writing and publishing an expert book for your perfect customer to automate your sales and marketing.

Why is this better than any other marketing tool? It's all you'll ever need. You put in minimal effort after it's done, and you'll keep attracting perfect customers to your business for years to come. I can't think of any better way to market a business that is more cost-effective or time efficient.

In chapter two, we are going to show you exactly how to use an expert book to make more money in any business. Few people understand the business model of using a book for marketing, but the ones who understand it, thrive.

In chapter three, we will cover the mistakes that most experts make that cause them to write the wrong book. Not only does this cost them time, energy, and money, but it still leaves them with the problem of trying to figure out how to get more clients.

Chapter four explains how to leverage your author status and use your book to virtually eliminate your competition. When you follow the advice here, no one else in your market will be able to touch you.

Chapters five and six are really important because they get into the nitty-gritty of using your book to attract leads that come to you ready to buy. You'll see how the right book will actually get people to upsell themselves and spend more money in your business.

You will find chapter seven to be a huge relief because it will reassure you that once you have your expert book, you really can just leave your marketing on autopilot. You just don't need to worry about doing any other marketing strategies.

Chapter eight shows you how good it can be when you know you have set things up so that your sales and marketing are handled. It really can be true. You just focus on your passion and do what you love, and the money just follows.

Chapter nine is for those of you who want to get into some of the more advanced stuff. We have shared our ten favorite strategies for using an expert book to make big money in your business.

Finally, for those of you who need to know how to do this and just want to get it done, chapter ten tells you just that. Most importantly, we're going to give you examples of exactly how we have brought in literally hundreds of thousands of dollars extra income each year using our book. You'll see how people in a variety of professions and industries have used their books to expand their business and increase their bottom line.

CHAPTER 2:
HOW A BOOK MAKES YOU MORE MONEY IN ANY BUSINESS

"Positioning yourself with a book builds your expert authority and trust—especially important since people always buy from people they know, like, and trust."

"If you hand out one hundred copies of your book to your potential perfect customers, it's literally impossible for you to not get business."

Bob:

The purpose of a business is to make money, and the purpose of marketing is to get customers. But, the big problem is that a lot of us end up in business almost by default or accident, especially if we are professionals.

You've gone to a professional school. Maybe you're a lawyer, a doctor, a chiropractor, or an optometrist, and you end up having to open up shop. Perhaps you saw a need that you could fulfill with a product or a certain way of using specific products and services. You're an expert who is passionate about helping people. You have skills and expertise where you've been trained for years.

You know you can help a lot of people, and you can help them get really great results, but how do you get those people? All of a sudden, you're faced with the fact that you need to get into marketing and selling when you never had any experience in that, you never got any training in it, and you really don't like it. You don't want to do it.

So how do you get around the fact that you're now a salesperson? Well, the beauty of having a book and being an author is that your book will do the sales and marketing for you, no matter what business you're in. Whether you're in a professional office or a service industry, whether you're in sales, insurance, or real estate, a book will work. Even if you have a store or sell products, your business can use this strategy.

If you position yourself with a book and really identify how you can help that client and transform their life, handing out your book is just an obvious way of connecting with them on an emotional level. They will start working with you.

We've seen it time and time again in all these industries. When you hand out your book for free, you're going to get more clients. If you hand out one hundred copies of your book to your potential perfect customers, it's literally impossible for you to not get business.

For example, one time in San Diego, I was at one of my mentor's events when I handed my book, 101 Reasons Why You Must Write a Book, to Kay White, a workplace communications expert. KayWhite.com It was my first book on how and why to write a book.

She read it on the plane back to London, England. She called me when she got home and said that she knew by the fifth reason that she wanted to write a book and needed my help.

We guided her as to the best way to write her 'how to be an influential communicator' book, The A to Z of Being Understood, made it a bestseller in London, and now she does very well handing out her books.

She was routinely closing $10,000.00 to $15,000.00 worth of business per speaking gig. She regularly gives everyone in the audience a copy of her book when she speaks. By adding the book to her speaking strategy, she was amazed to see that the long-term payoff from speaking engagements often topped six figures. Her book is a credibility-builder and a door-opener to both private and corporate clients.

As a matter of fact, I've handed out a single book on occasion and followed up with that one person. The amount of business that came from that one client has now been over six figures.

The opportunities are always there, but you have to hand out your book. That's why we always say, "Hand out your book for free. Don't worry about the ten or twenty dollars. Focus on the big numbers you're going to get by working with your ideal clients and your perfect customers."

Dr. Paul:

It was pretty amazing the first day that our book came off the presses. I had just received a few boxes of books, and I was so proud of it that I just wanted to give it to everyone.

I work from home, and I need to have some sort of social interaction during the day, so I make sure I get out to the gym. I handed my book to the gym owner. I just said, "Hey Alfie, here's my new book."

He looked at it and said, "Wow! I'm going to get you to write my book."

I went in and did a 45-minute workout. When I came back out, he said, "I'm serious, Paul. Can we talk?"

We set up a meeting the very next week. By the end of that meeting, I had a $10,000.00 client.

That was the first book that I handed out. Since then, we have done hundreds of thousands of dollars just from that one book, and it just continues to keep working for us.

Here are the things that will happen to you when you get your expert book written and published:

1. You'll find a client in the most unexpected place.

2. People will be so impressed that they will brag about you.

3. You'll get asked to speak to a group about your expertise.

4. People you've been wanting to connect with will call you.

5. You'll be asked for interviews.

6. TV and radio opportunities will open up to you.

7. People will start buying more from you without you having to ask.

8. You'll feel like a celebrity.

If you hand your book to one hundred perfect customers, and it states exactly what their problem is and the perfect solution they want, you cannot help but get business. If you get into organizations and associations where your perfect customers hang out, and you give out as many books as they need, the referrals you will get will just pay you back in spades. Your books will be passed around, and you'll even get calls from people who were given your book by someone else. You will find business coming in from the strangest places.

The Secret Power of Storytelling

One of the best things you can do in your book is tell stories. Stories create an emotional connection with people. When you tell your own story, the story of your business, and success stories of your clients, people get drawn in. They feel like they know you. Positioning yourself with a book builds your expert authority and trust. People always buy from people they know, like, and trust.

Another reason the stories you tell are absolutely amazing, is that people won't remember facts and figures, but they will remember the story and how you made them feel. That's exactly what personal stories and accounts of your clients' successes do for you.

Bob Mangat is in the marketing business. His company, Invigo Media (InvigoMedia.com), helps doctors, specialists, and pain practitioners set up their automated marketing campaigns. He creates their Facebook ads and sets up their online marketing to get them leads.

The funny thing is that while he is the online marketing guru, he still sees the value of a book for generating business. We helped him write his book, The Automated Entrepreneur, which he gives away any time he speaks, networks, or attends events that his perfect customers go to.

At one particular event, Bob was talking to a pain practitioner who had ten locations in the United States. He was very successful and seemed to have his marketing down. He and Bob really connected and ended up having dinner together. They parted ways, and Bob was not expecting anything to come of it.

The very next morning, Bob got a call from the guy saying, "I read your book on my flight home. I want you to do what you said in your book for all ten of my locations."

This turned into a contract worth $30,000.00 a month. It was all because his book did the work for him after the guy had said he did not need Bob's services.

Even if you don't think you have any good stories, there is always a way to tell a story to make it compelling. I'm always surprised by the stories people reveal right after they tell me they don't have any good stories.

Dr. Daniel Mashoof, a holistic dentist in Seattle, (DrDanielMashoof.com) was struggling to dig up success stories that would make him stand out. After prodding him for a few minutes, I found lots of emotionally charged stories.

One lady was so traumatized by the fact that her twin sister had had to be hospitalized after having a mercury filling removed, that she flew in from out of state to get him to do the procedure safely.

Another lady was suffering from a strange illness that had resulted in the loss of her left eye. She was terrified. Doctors and specialists couldn't make any sense of it, and the symptoms progressed. A naturopath made the connection between her illness and the two root canals in her mouth. He referred her to Dr. Daniel. The day after he had safely removed the affected teeth, all her symptoms disappeared.

Do you think people will respond more to these stories than to a long, boring doctor's narrative about how mercury and other substances affect your health? Of course they will! When other people find that patients fly in from out of state to see Dr. Daniel to get these results, they will, too.

If you haven't grabbed our CEA Storytelling Template yet, go to CelebrityExpertAuthor.com/Templates to download it now. It will walk you through the steps we use to turn our clients' boring stories into gripping and emotional stories. Start gathering your own compelling success stories for your book now. It will inspire you and help you to write a book that draws your perfect customers right in.

Most of the time, people are so used to the results that they get with their clients that they don't really see them as anything special. They don't describe the results in the way that their clients see them. They end up telling a boring story and waste a great opportunity to connect with someone emotionally and get a new client.

The best thing about a good story is that your readers will even repeat them long after they have forgotten what your book is about. Most experts want to talk about their expertise and the statistics about their products and services when they start writing their book. They want to talk about how their approach is better and explain how their services work.

A good book uses real-life examples to show the results in action. Readers don't care about the stats. They want to know what their life will look like when they get the results. The best way to show them this is by showing them someone else who got what they want.

We fell into the trap of explaining too much with our last book, How to Be a Celebrity Expert Author. We were heavy on the information and the "how to" of writing your book and building your business.

How to Be a Celebrity Expert Author has worked incredibly well, and continues to generate very lucrative business for us. As we have worked with clients to produce their books, we have focused on showing their information in action through examples and stories. We started to feel that the books we were producing were so good that we thought we could do a better job for ourselves. That is what sparked this book.

The connection you get through stories is what really helps you to write the right book: a book that attracts the perfect customer, creates rapport, and makes them say, "They're talking to me. That's exactly what I want. They can help me."

You want to make sure your expert book has that effect. Otherwise, the time, effort, and money you put into it won't have the impact and return that you want.

It's sad to see people write the wrong book. It's so easy to connect with clients through stories and have your book do the marketing and sales for you. Ultimately, it all comes down to sales. That's why we're in business and that's why we're doing marketing. We have to prospect, we have to get leads, and we have to sell. If we don't turn those leads into customers, our business suffers.

But hey, most of us didn't get into business because we wanted to be marketing and sales people. We wanted to help people with our products and services.

> Being a chiropractor, I know this for a fact. I loved helping people in pain heal and watching how they could turn their lives around just by coming into my office. I didn't want to go out there looking for these people, and I definitely didn't want to have to pitch them. It was so painful for me to sit down and talk to people about the money, but I was in business, and that's what I had to do.

A lot of professionals find themselves in this same situation, and that is why we're telling you to write your expert book. When you're an author, it keeps people focused on your status and expertise. You don't have to be the salesman anymore because your book does the sales for you. You're viewed as an elite person in society, a knowledgeable expert. You have status and people look up to you. They are actually coming to you for who you are, rather than what you do. They will make decisions emotionally because you are an author, the leading expert, and you have expertise that can help them. They won't shop around and they won't bat an eye at your prices.

Another great benefit of writing the right book is that you can make it unsell the clients you don't want. Early on in practice, there was a time where I would just see anybody and everybody. I was bending over backward for people that I really hated working with. I was afraid to lose them because I didn't want the money to walk out the door.

By writing your book to tell people exactly how you work with them to get results, the people who are willing to follow your process will become customers, and the ones who aren't, won't. When you fill your business with perfect customers that you love working with, who want what you offer, and spend the money to get great results, work doesn't feel like work anymore. You become very attractive, and people will want to bring their friends and family. All you have to do is give your book to these happy customers and they will pass it on to their friends and family. They'll brag about how great you are, and your business just snowballs.

Being an expert author sets you apart in your field. You stand out from all the other people with the same credentials or those who do or offer the same thing you do. You no longer have to compete with them on price because there is no comparing apples to apples. They will see good reason to invest in your product or service, because they know you're the best. This just allows you to get more leads and close more sales without having to do any work.

The best way to be the leading expert in your field is to become the specialist. This is done by choosing a specific aspect of a broader subject to focus on, and then specializing in it. Think about this in medicine. Specialists like cardiologists, neurologists, or orthopedic surgeons make way more money than general practitioners (GPs). They are much more highly respected, have a waiting list, and can only be seen with a referral from a GP. When you position yourself properly with your book, you become the specialist.

Being the specialist can make marketing really easy. You don't have to go posting on social media every single day about what you're doing. You don't have to go out networking, work out your elevator pitch, or exchange cards. You just keep on passing out your book and letting it do all the hard work. As a result, you become known as the leading expert, and even your colleagues and competitors will refer to you.

People have used this strategy of narrowing their niche and being the specialist in all different kinds of businesses. When you use an expert book to focus on a perfect customer and you proclaim that you are the specialist in solving their biggest problem, you will see your bottom line increase—a lot of the times, dramatically. When you have the right book written with stories about the results that your perfect customer wants, as long as you keep giving it out, clients will keep coming in.

Candace Plattor (CandacePlattor.com), is a really great addictions therapist. She positioned herself with an expert book and became a specialist who works with the families of drug addicts to help them heal.

Just imagine the pain of having someone that you love destroying their lives by using dangerous substances. This causes so much emotional pain and financial destruction in families. Candace is so good at getting families to heal the pain behind the addiction that loved ones get their lives back, whole families come back together, and in many cases, the addicts stop using and begin to heal.

When we met her, she had a very full practice and was taking on as many clients as she wanted. But she felt that she was working too hard. She was at a point in her life where she did not want to keep working at that pace. She was already charging at least $100.00 more an hour than every other therapist in the area—and she was getting it. That's how it is for specialists.

When we heard about her results, we told her that she could easily be charging the same price that people pay for rehab. She balked because a month in rehab is easily $25,000.00 to $35,000.00 for a month—and these people weren't even getting better. She was getting people better.

We showed her how to use her author status to sell her services as a program for $20,000.00 (a bargain when you consider that lives are at stake). She was really good at relating to her clients' emotional pain and telling stories of the successes that she had.

It only took her a month to wrap her head around what we showed her, and she got three new clients in her program within the next ten days. She made $60,000.00, which is almost 60 percent of what she had been making in a year!

That's what happens when you position yourself with the right book: a book that is written for the purpose of generating leads and referrals, and closing high-end customers. This is exactly what we'll be showing you throughout the rest of this book.

CHAPTER 3:

WHY THE RIGHT BOOK IS CRITICAL & THE WRONG BOOK WILL GATHER DUST ON YOUR SHELF

". . . the right book for marketing your business and increasing your bottom line by attracting perfect customers is all about your customers."

Dr. Paul:

The biggest mistake most experts make when they write their expert book is they write the wrong book. Now, there are a lot of reasons to write a book, but the only reason that we're going to focus on here is promoting your business and making money. Beginning with that goal in mind, when you start writing, you will get on the right track.

There are many things that will make or break your book. We don't want to make a big investment of time, energy, and money for a personal trophy that sits on our shelf and gathers dust. We only want to put in the effort once and have it work for us for years to come. You are building a marketing tool that will make you thousands and thousands of dollars with little effort after it is written.

We can't stress this enough. You must keep your eyes on the right numbers if you want to make good money with a book. There is no money in selling books. Eighty percent of the authors on The New York Times' Best Sellers list have full-time jobs to pay their bills. Marketing and selling your book is focusing on the wrong numbers. The average royalty on a book is about $1.00; even if you sell 30,000 copies, you can't live very long on that amount.

This is the biggest mistake that most entrepreneurial authors make: they put too much effort into marketing their book. They invest time, energy, and money to promote and sell their books. Even if you make book sales yourself and keep the full $20.00 from the sale, you're missing out on the big money. So, listen up! This is the big secret to making really big money with your book. Give it away! Anyone and everyone who could become your perfect customer needs a copy of your expert book.

Think about it. What is the lifetime value of your perfect customer? For most experts, business owners and professionals, it is easily in the hundreds of thousands of dollars. The big money is in the products and services that your business provides. Use your book to market your business.

A colleague of mine, another chiropractor, had written ten five books. They were about nutrition, well-being, and his expertise in vitamins and supplements. I was really impressed until he told me that he had not made any money from them. The problem was that he was focusing on the wrong numbers.

These books were sitting in his office—in a nice display, of course—available for sale. He complained that his patients would say, "That's great. Can I have a copy?" He thought that there was too much value in the time and effort he had spent writing them to give them away.

It took him years of effort to produce these books. The tens of thousands of dollars he had spent were making a net return of $0.00. If he had put a book into the hand of every client and sent them out the door with it, they would be bragging about him and passing that book on to their friends and family. And if he had written the books with the intention of using them to get patients and capitalize on the lifetime value of a patient, he only would have had to write one book, and his investment would have paid dividends for years to come.

Bob:

One of our clients is a trichologist, which is someone who is trained to diagnose the causes of hair loss. She can, in many cases, reverse the condition. She had written a book all about different situations that cause hair loss, and even showed microscopic pictures of the hair follicle problems that were causing the condition.

She was so focused on educating people about the causes of hair loss that she missed what was truly the key to making a fortune growing back hair naturally. Her book was priced at $69.95 because she thought this was such valuable information that people losing their hair needed to know.

She was struggling in a business that should have been thriving. We got her to see that her perfect customers—women—were in a lot of pain due to the shame and embarrassment of losing their hair. They did not care why their hair follicles weren't growing hair. They just wanted to grow it back so they could get their lives back!

When she got her head wrapped around this, she stopped charging $250.00 for a treatment and started selling $10,000.00 hair regrowth packages. She now gives her book away to potential clients and referral partners to build her authority in the area of natural hair regrowth. While it does not speak to her perfect customers' problems, it does make her the specialist in the competitive hairloss industry.

What's even more interesting is that she had seen me speak three years earlier in Phoenix at an event. I'd given her a copy of my book and she held onto it for all that time before she finally called me and became a client. Just another perfect example of how giving out a book at a talk keeps working for you and can bring you business even three years later.

Stories really get people hyped up on your business. First of all, your perfect customer is never going to remember any of the stats, and they don't want to listen to any of your legalese, technical jargon, or doctor talk. The only thing that they're going to remember is how you made them feel. Did you connect to them emotionally? The way to do that is through story.

Another great benefit of a good story is that people will often share it with their friends. It's like you're training all of your future sales people by telling that initial client a memorable and emotional story. We all tell stories, just like the story about the trichologist, and the fact that she came to me three years after getting my book. It's those stories we remember, and a powerful story really does the selling for you.

Think about your patients or your clients telling your stories, parroting them to other people. If it left an impression on them, it will impress the friends they tell too. Then perfect prospects turn into perfect customers.

Dr. Paul:

The first thing you want to do when you start writing your book, is to write down your ten biggest success stories—what stands out in your mind as the most amazing transformations you've have gotten for your clients. Oftentimes, experts don't even think that what they've done is that impressive. That's why we have to really dig for and mine out these stories. Use our CEA Storytelling Template, available at CelebrityExpertAuthor.com/Templates, to help you.

It can simply be a matter of looking at the results through the eyes of your perfect customer, from their perspective and seeing how transformative or life-changing the results are in their world. That's how we turn a ho-hum account that people find really boring into an amazing story that draws people in and makes them say, "I want that!" This way, we can really see the value of the story, and we turn something that the client thinks is really boring into something really amazing.

Candace Plattor, the addictions therapist, could not imagine people paying $20,000.00 to work with her until she looked at her results through her client's eyes. She just described the pain through their point of view. Lending an addict money, the emotional blackmail, being up all night worrying if they're alive, losing jobs, the lies and deceit.

When she started telling the story of how devastating it is for a family to be ripped apart by drugs or alcohol, she had no problem asking for the amount and getting paid. We are still encouraging her to raise her prices because she is not charging near enough.

That's the way to write your book to position your business and show your perfect customers how you can help them.

Unfortunately, most authors sink themselves because they think that what they do and what they know is interesting. They write a book that is all about themselves and is only interesting to. . . you guessed it! Themselves. And that is how you write the wrong book.

For that matter, it doesn't just apply to what you write in your book. You shouldn't bore your customers like that when you talk to them, either. I was guilty of that for years in practice. I thought that the spine and nerves were amazing and that everyone should know about how their nerves control everything in your body. I would do classes explaining exactly how a chiropractor helps your nervous system so you can have optimal nerve function.

Fortunately for my sake, people are really polite and smile and nod even though they don't have a clue or care about what you're saying.

The stressed-out mom with debilitating back pain wanted to hear about other moms that had a newborn and kids that needed to go to soccer. She would have been more impressed to hear about how it only took a week of chiropractic treatment before those other moms could pick up their babies again and manage their household without having a nervous breakdown.

Meanwhile, I was talking about the nervous system and why everyone needs lifelong chiropractic care for optimal health.

The guy next to her was worried about whether he would be able to play golf this season because of his neck. All he wanted to know was that he would be better soon, and that my other golfers have been able to play even better because they have no more pain and have even better motion in their swing.

When I learned to tell good stories, I got a lot more new patients out of my talks. And that's the point of telling great stories in your book, too. Most expert authors talk all about the technical aspects of what they do. They think legalese, doctorese, or tech talk makes them sound smart and impresses people. The opposite is actually true. When you use big, fancy words beyond people's comprehension, they get turned off and you actually push them away.

The best way to write is in normal, conversational language. Describe what you do by talking about situations they can relate to. Explain the results, the outcomes, the benefits, or the transformation that they're going to have in their life. Describe this with examples of how much happier their family life is going to be.

Don't just say they will be happy and fulfilled. Tell them what it's like to wake up for the first time without pain, what it looks like when they finally get the solution they have been looking for. When you describe what you do this way, you will never have to convince people to buy your product or service. They will sell themselves.

Another place where authors sink themselves is by writing a book that's full of personal stories that people don't relate to. They think they're interesting, but most of their clients don't. They might have lived a horrific life and come a long way, but their clients just don't want to hear it. Your clients are paying money to you and they've come to you for a reason. All they care about is, "What's in it for me?" And they should.

So if you're talking about yourself, make sure it's brief and that it always relates to something that your customers want for themselves. The more that we're aware of this as service professionals, entrepreneurs, and practitioners, the more we tune into the fact that our stories really communicate what's in it for them. If they think that the book is all about the author, you lose them very quickly. You can tell stories about yourself as long as the people reading the story will relate to it and see themselves in the story. It has to make them want to get your assistance to get the same outcome you got.

A speaker once gave me his book at an author event I attended. He wanted to use it to build his motivational speaking business. It was one horrific story after another about accidents and near-death experiences. And that's all it was. He thought it would motivate people to find the good in their lives.

When I asked him how people were responding to it, he said that they found it too traumatic and could not relate. The time, money, and effort that it had taken to write and publish that book had all been wasted.

Bob:

So the right book for marketing your business and increasing your bottom line by attracting perfect customers is all about them. It tells about the benefits you can give them from their perspective. It uses stories and examples rather than jargon and boring narrative to make your points.

There's a sweet spot for the size of this type of book. When you're focusing on giving your book away as marketing, rather than selling your book for a tiny profit, this is really important. If your book is too long, you've written the wrong book.

When Paul and I speak to audiences of twenty-five, fifty, or one hundred people, everybody in that audience gets a free book. Every time we do that, we get business. Every single time. No exceptions. With larger audiences, we can often negotiate with the event organizer to pay for all or part of the cost of the books.

Even if you're stuck with the whole bill, it's still the cheapest marketing for the biggest return. If a hundred or more of your perfect customers have your marketing book in their hands and they hear you speak, there is absolutely no way to not get clients. At an average cost of $6.00 to $8.00 per 120-page book, that's only $600.00 to $800.00 to give an audience of one hundred people your book.

Now, you may be thinking, "Whoa! I'm giving away $600.00 to $800.00 worth of books." But you'll always get back your return on investment many, many times over. Just refer back to the lifetime value of a perfect customer if you have any doubts.

Whereas, if you focus on selling it and making a couple of dollars a book, the right people that could become perfect customers, that should have the book in their hands may not want to spend the $20.00. Meanwhile, if you give them a copy of that book, there's the law of reciprocity. They are grateful and they feel indebted to you.

So the sweet spot is 120 pages. If you go shorter than that, it will look more like a report or fancy brochure. At 120 pages, it has the look and feel of an actual book, but it's a lot lighter than a 380-page book. This is good if you're hauling a bunch of them around with you or flying with them. The cost to print stays down, which is good because you want to be giving away as many as you possibly can. A 380-page book will cost you two to three times as much to print. While it's the best return on investment for marketing, it still never hurts to be frugal.

This size (120 pages) is good for keeping shipping costs and postage down when you send them out to potential customers. When I mail our book from Canada, I can send it in a bubble wrap envelope as an oversized letter. This costs $3.00 within Canada, $5.00 to the United States, and $10.00 overseas. Any bigger and it is considered a package, and the costs skyrocket.

You're not writing a Pulitzer Prize-winning book. This is about writing a book that gets your message out and communicates it really clearly to your perfect customer through story. We're a very busy society. There are so many things trying to grab our attention right now. If you can communicate your story in 120 pages, people can read it before they go to work, during lunch, or after dinner. It's an easy read.

> I love the topic of the law of attraction. This one fellow caught my attention with a really great YouTube video on the subject. I have read lots of books about the law of attraction, so when this guy said he had a book I thought, "Jeez, I should buy that book."
>
> I went to straight to Amazon and found out it was 480 pages. I hit the brakes right there. I don't have the time to read a 480-page book.

Another factor that is critical in writing the right book is your publisher. You have to find a publisher who works with you to publish a book with the look and feel that will resonate with your perfect customers. While it has to make you look really good, it also must reel in the people you want to serve in your business.

The Three Kinds of Publishers

There are three kinds of publishers out there right now:

1. Traditional publishing houses (like Penguin and Hay House)

2. Self-publishing companies

3. Pay-to-publish companies

The traditional publishing houses have gone the way of the dinosaur. There are very few of them and they are out to make money from book sales. When it comes to taking on an author, they only take calculated risks.

If you think your topic is the next big thing and they should take a chance on you, here's what calculated risk means. If they look at you and they think that your book is going to make them a lot of money, they're probably going to publish your book. But for most of us mere mortals, we don't have the following (unlike Oprah or Deepak Chopra) that they're going to make money on in royalties.

I've seen a person with a million-person following get turned down because there was not enough profit in it. The traditional publishing route has almost completely evaporated. If you're looking for a traditional publishing contract, you have a better chance of growing a third eye and being struck by lightning in it.

Then there is self-publishing. With technology these days, a lot of different options have become very available to anybody and everybody. You can go online and find exactly how to get your book published and distributed on Amazon yourself. There are a number of steps to take and there is a steep learning curve in doing this. There are courses you can take and people you can hire to help you do this if you want invest the time and effort. You could also figure out how to build a car, if you wanted, but it's just not going to be as good or as safe.

However, there are so many mistakes that you can make that make you look really bad. Everyone can tell a self-published book, and even when you work with some of the self-publishing companies, people just don't see it as very professional. So it really pays you to have a professionally published book.

If the traditional publishing house is not an option for you, and you don't want to waste your time and energy figuring out how to be a publisher, then the third option, pay-to-publish companies, is probably for you. Paying a publisher for professional publishing and a good name can do a lot for your image, which is what you wanted to do with your book in the first place. Isn't it?

You want to be careful here, because not all pay-to-publish publishers are created equal. You can hire any number of companies to publish your book for you, which actually just means getting it into print and out there. However, if you want a book that markets your business and closes sales, you want a publisher who understands the concept of using your book as a marketing tool. A company that is more about marketing than publishing, really.

If you run a business all day, you don't want to be spending your time at night trying to figure this out. Writing and publishing this kind of book and getting it generating money for you is something you can do in ninety days. Some do it faster, but most people take about six months.

Once you have your book done—you've written the right book and you've had it professionally published—now we can look at using the book to generate leads and be the leading expert. It will actually make you stand out from all the people in your field that do exactly the same thing, even if they're right down the street from you. It will have people spending more money with you, for exactly the same service your competitors offer.

CHAPTER 4:

HOW TO USE YOUR BOOK TO BE THE LEADING EXPERT & STAND OUT FROM THE COMPETITION

"Author status immediately expands your sphere of influence, elevates your authority, and gives you an edge over all your competitors."

Dr. Paul:

In today's market, people like to shop around. They're trying to compare apples to apples, and they're looking for the best price. They can be really frustrating to deal with because you just can't compare quality, results, and service. Most business owners feel that if they just had a chance to explain what they offered and the specific benefits, that people would make a wiser buying choice. But people are so wary of being sold to that they are suspicious of free offers or no-obligation consultations. It's hard to even get someone to talk to you.

The good news is that you can get around all this when you're the author of the book on the subject. In fact, you don't even have to make any special offers to get people to want to talk to you. Author status immediately expands your sphere of influence, elevates your authority, and gives you an edge over all your competitors. You get a taste of celebrity status. Your reputation precedes you. People just have an irrational affinity toward you.

Let's talk about what having a book actually does for your business. When a potential client receives a book about you and your business, all their objections get handled with zero risk to them. By the time they get to you, their suspicions have been put to rest.

Writing and publishing a book on a topic automatically makes you the authority in that area. And because most people think it's too hard to do, nobody else does it. But when you know how simple it can be and how quickly you could establish your author advantage, you can really set yourself apart from any of your competition.

When your sphere of influence increases (which happens instantly when you write a book), people actually treat you differently. When celebrities endorse certain products, such as a celebrity on TV going on about the amazing effects of a brand of toothpaste, people buy into the celebrity's influence, even though they have absolutely no expertise in dentistry. When you become an author, you get that same sort of influence over people.

By becoming an authority figure, people are paying you more for who you are than for what you do. This is an incredibly lucrative position to be in. The higher paid a person is, the more they are paid for who they are than for what they do.

If you want to charge prices way above the market rate, the only way to do it is by building up who you are, increasing your sphere of influence, and getting celebrity status. Sometimes, years of experience and results can do this, but the fastest way is to write an expert book.

Gobinder Gill (GobinderGill.com) was no stranger to struggles due to racial prejudice. He was brought to Canada from India, an orphan at age nine. His focus and determination made him a name in radio and television, but his background left him wanting to contribute to society in a bigger way.

Gobinder became an advocate for diversity in the workplace and positioned himself with his Amazon #1 Best Seller, Achieving Prosperity through Diversity. He is hired to speak across Canada and the United States, and commands fees upwards of $7,500.00 per hour.

It even works if you're the new kid on the block and you don't have years of experience under your belt. Maybe you're new in the field and you have no years of experience like a brand new chiropractor, doctor, or dentist fresh out of school. People are wondering why should they trust you when the guy down the street has fifteen or twenty years on you and a reputation.

Jon Simcoe (LionOpportunities.com) is a real estate investor and an expert in the rent-to-own market. Because he became an entrepreneur at such an early age (he started his first business at 12), people sometimes question his credibility and success based on his young appearance.

A potential investor was doing just that as she pondered the decision to put money into one of Jon's opportunities. Jon's assistant handed the lady his Amazon #1 Best Selling book, The Rent to Own Solution to Home Ownership, and said, "This is why he knows what he's doing." The lady signed the check.

People put a lot of weight on credentials, and they invest a lot of time and money to get them. For me, becoming a chiropractor took eight years of schooling, and hundreds of thousands of dollars of investment in tuition and money lost from not generating income for all those years.

Many people hold back on doing what they really want to do in business and offering what they want, because they don't feel like they have the right credentials. With a book, you give yourself your own credentials and claim your authority in that area immediately. It's the highest earned form of credibility.

All the medical students that complete med school become doctors, but very few of them go on to be authors. Even within professions, becoming an author elevates your status further. As a chiropractor, I enjoyed a certain amount of respect and credibility as a doctor, but as soon as I became an author, people were interested in me on a whole new level.

Another factor that you absolutely need but just can't buy is trust. People only buy from people they know, like, and trust. They just don't buy from strangers. When you write a book, you can gain trust almost immediately, because you wrote the book on that particular topic. Of course, acting in integrity is critical, but there's no other way to gain that trust as quickly.

When you become the leading authority, you're no longer a stranger. If somebody has received a copy of your book and read about you and why you are a leader in the field, you instantly gain their respect. It gives you an advantage over all the other people they are trying to choose from—everyone online offering the best services, results, or prices. It's not rational. It's just because you wrote a book about it.

When you write the right book, you can use your author status to build trust and attract clients to your business. Health professionals often offer free consultations or maybe a free exam. It's a very popular way to attract new patients.

It's been found that offering a free book versus a free consultation gets a better response in attracting new patients. People who receive a book and then come to a free consultation are far more likely to become patients than if they just received a free consultation alone. Everyone knows that nothing is free. They see the free exam offer as a sales ploy to get them into the office and sell them.

People don't like being sold, but they do like to buy. When you offer a free book that explains the solution to their problem and gives options to solve it, they feel they are receiving value. Books are perceived as a source of knowledge and information. When people come in through your book, they're much higher quality clients. A client who comes in through your book will stay three times longer, spend three times more, and refer you ten times more often.

The offer for a free consultation can also be made from the book once they have established that sort of rapport with you as an author. There's no other source that's going to give you more valuable clients. You're basically getting the benefit of offering a free consultation, but you're taking out the risk to them.

The marketplace is getting more and more competitive as more people are offering the same products and services. It's so easy for people to shop around for price online, making it harder and harder to stand out.

The last thing that you want to do is compete on price, so the best option is to become the leading expert. And a book elevates your status so people see you as the authority. Offering to send out a free book on your website and anywhere else people may come across you builds this no-risk rapport with them. When your competitors are handing out business cards and brochures, and you're giving your book as your business card, choosing you becomes a no-brainer.

Many people fall into the trap of thinking they need more training or that they must go back to school for certifications and designations. Nowadays, people don't even really see degrees. BAs, MAs, and PhDs are all just a jumble of letters. The title "doctor" does give you some credibility, but information is so readily available, people will question even a doctor. Writing your book is a way quicker and far more powerful way to gain authority and respect than spending time and money on credentials.

When you have positioned yourself with a book in a competitive marketplace, you can raise your prices while everybody else is lowering them to compete. By featuring your expertise, the processes you use, your different products, and the specific benefits your perfect customers seek, people see the value in paying more. They will be willing to pay you for who you are, rather than for what you do.

One of the biggest problems in business is commoditization. Live by price, die by price. There's only so much you can cut costs. It's a war you will always lose. Positioning yourself as the authority with a book gets you totally out of that commodity race. You never want to be stuck in the "compare apples to apples, justify your price" situation.

In health professions or other regulated professions, there are often a lot of rules about how you can market. As a chiropractor, my college and regulatory board would say, "You can't make certain claims about results. You can't talk about your successes. You can't claim to be an expert in a certain area."

But you can certainly talk about all these things in your expert book. You may not be allowed to use testimonials in your marketing, but you can put as many success stories as you want in your book. Then, when you use your book as marketing for your business, you get around all the regulations imposed on you.

There are so many advantages to having your book do your marketing for you. It's a very powerful tool when you're in a highly regulated industry. Not only does a book help people to choose you over your competitors, it makes it a lot easier for you to make much bigger sales.

In the next chapter, we're going to explain why a book helps professionals, business owners, and entrepreneurs sell bigger and better packages or services. When you're passionate about what you do but hate being a salesperson, a book is exactly what you need. You just let it do the work: getting you great customers, upselling them, and closing them on big sales.

CHAPTER 5:
HOW A BOOK MAKES CLOSING HIGH-PRICED SALES A DONE DEAL

"Your book tells customers all about your products or
services, the benefits to them, and why making the
investment is a good idea.
Customers don't feel like you are selling them;
they feel like they are getting to know you."

Oftentimes, for a client to get the best outcome or results, they must make a significant investment in your product or services. Professionals are sometimes wary of saying how much they charge, because they worry that the price tag will scare off prospective customers.

The beauty of an expert book is that you can showcase your product or service offerings from low-end to high-end, and explain the benefits and shortcomings of each. Ultimately, the customer usually wants the best, and you end up closing a higher-priced sale.

Let's get into how this works. When your book explains the value and benefits of your products or services, it explains or justifies your prices so you don't have to. Don't we always think, "If they knew what we knew, they'd do what we do"?

So often, if we just take the time to explain the benefits and long-term results of investing a little more, they buy a bigger package or a higher level of service. People don't like being sold to, but they do like to buy. When your book does the explaining for you and the decision is left up to them, they upsell themselves.

People are so skeptical and they don't want to be sold to. A book gives them a no-risk way of checking out what you do or exactly what you have to offer. It's acting as your unpaid salesperson, and you have the confidence of knowing that it's saying what you want, the way you want it said.

If you're expecting your customers to spend a lot of money with you, they need to know, like, and trust you. They usually need to be referred or to know you first. You can't buy trust, and people won't buy from strangers. Trust is earned over a long period of time. But if your book creates the trust factor, that time period is very much shortened. Being an author builds the trust factor quickly, and in ways that you just can't do with other forms of lead generation.

When people are out to spend a large sum of money, they want to do some research. A book can help them a lot with that. When a person is doing research, they're obviously a very serious buyer. They're not just going to buy the first thing that they see; they're researching it.

Where do people turn? To the Internet, but they know they can't trust everything they see online. However, when you Google a subject, books on Amazon also come up in the search. So if you know your perfect customer well and you know what they are searching for, your book comes up in that search, too. And a book packs a lot more credibility than random information posted on the web. If they've gone to the trouble of searching for a book on your particular topic or niche, they're not only a buyer, they're a good buyer.

They're the clients you want. They will be the easiest to work with. They will come to you because of who you are, your expert status, your authority, and the fact that they trust you. People that come through your book are the ones that you want to foster as clients, and they're definitely the best clients to have. And we can't stress enough that these people stay three times longer, spend three times more, and refer ten times more often.

Livia Pellerin (LiviaPellerin.com) is a structural integration therapist. She helps athletes and CrossFitters heal from injuries and get in tune with their bodies while improving their mobility as well as their mental outlook. Her bodywork requires a series of ten sessions, and she was having trouble getting clients to commit to the process and follow through.

She positioned herself with her forthcoming book, Your Desire Genius, and used her expert status to sell clients $1,150.00 bodywork packages and $3,000.00 coaching packages. That very week, she closed $10,000.00 in sales. (Her prior month billings were only $2,000.00.)

When it comes down to the actual price of the investment, we have to be aware of who the decision-maker in the
family is. There is often a spouse involved in money-mak-
ing decisions. Often, the potential customer has to go home
and attempt to explain again (usually badly) what you've told
them and justify your price to the decision-maker.

The neat thing is, you can now say to them, "I understand that you want to talk to your spouse to get a decision,
and I think that's a good idea. Why don't you give them this
signed copy of my book, and discuss it with them tonight?"
You set up another meeting for the next day and let your
book make the close for you.

By knowing that the book will actually close the sale for
you, you can almost "unsell." If they have objections, you
don't have to push the issue. You don't have to try to close
the sale. You can just say, "It's not a problem. Take the book
and read through it with your spouse. Then you can make
the decision."

That decision will be made through the book, and you'll
have a good client. When it comes to upselling to higher levels of your product or service, you will always be glad to have
the options detailed in your book.

I was at my dentist's office getting my teeth cleaned
one day when I overheard him talking to another patient.
She had her mouth full of his hand, the suction tube, and
other tools while he was telling her about how well her
fillings and root canals were holding up. Then he started
telling her about crowns and implants. He talked about the
costs and told her to check her insurance so she could

decide on whether she wanted to pursue either of those options.

I was thinking, as the hygienist buffed my teeth, that if he had a book about the benefits of crowns and implants over filling and root canals, he would be selling people on way more of the much more profitable options.

Imagine if he had just said, "I think that it's time for you to make some decisions about your dental health. Here is my book outlining the different options, how they work, the procedure, and the costs of each. Read through it and next time you're in, we can talk about the best way for you to proceed." Many of his patients would be upselling themselves to crowns and implants.

When you lay out the product and service offering from high-end to low-end, people almost always want the best quality. When they have the chance to research on their own and read about it, they sell themselves. You aren't having to keep explaining the same things to all your clients, and you don't have to be a salesperson.

You can use the unsell process again. When they're not really sure whether they want to go to the next level, you don't have to push the issue. Just tell them to read the book over and discuss it with their spouse. Let the book do its work, and the next time they're in, most likely they will have upsold themselves.

Rather than making the decision based on cost, they're really thinking of the benefit for them. They read over the information in your expert book and think, "This makes so much sense. It really is worth the extra investment."

You're not trying to convince them to spend more money. They convince themselves. It's quite normal, once someone's read your book, for them to come in and say, "I want the whole deal."

It's amazing what happens when your book, with all the details of your products or services and benefits and success stories, ends up in the hands of a referral. When they make time to sit down with your book, it's as if they are scheduling a meeting with you. One of your clients gives your book to a referral, or you mail your book to a prospective client. When they read your book, they feel like they are checking you out with no risk to themselves. They're getting the information and they're making a buying decision.

Your book tells them all about your products or services, the benefits to them, and why making the investment is a good idea. They don't feel like you are selling them, but they feel like they are getting to know you. This is why, when they come in through your book, they don't come to check you out. They come to buy.

It's actually been shown that when chiropractors offer a free book versus a free exam, they get a higher quality of patient. They also get a higher number of people saying, "Yes, I want the free book," than people saying, "Yes, I want a free exam."

When people go in for a free consultation, they're skeptical because they know that you're going to try to sell them on something. But when they get your book, they feel like they received a gift, not a piece of marketing.

Your customers or your patients want to refer you, but they quite often just don't know how. Just like so many of us, they don't want to feel like a salesperson. The neat thing about a book is that they just have to pass it to that person. They will inevitably say something like, "Here's somebody you can use. I go too, and I think he's great. He's a friend of mine."

They will brag about you because people love to associate themselves with people who have a big sphere of influence. You're setting them up with a referral system that not only works, it makes it really easy for them to be your cheerleader.

Being a chiropractor, I know that once people know that chiropractic techniques are safe, comfortable, and effective, they enjoy going to their chiropractor. However, they like to brag about how their chiropractor contorts, twists, and cracks them and "breaks" their back. These are far from selling features for me!

It's really important to know what your customers are saying about you and your business if you want to get good referrals. When you have an expert book, you never have to worry about this because your book says exactly what you want that referral to know.

Ultimately, you want your book to end up in the hands of anyone and everyone who comes through your business. They need to have a copy of your book for their benefit, so they know how to utilize and purchase your products or services to get the best results. It's also great for them to pass on to somebody else.

It's really the cheapest investment you can make for the highest quality client. The beauty of a book is you make the investment of time, energy, and money once to produce it, and then you have a marketing piece that will pay you back for years to come. In fact, you may never have to do it again.

CHAPTER 6:

HOW TO GENERATE MORE QUALIFIED LEADS & REFERRALS WITH YOUR BOOK

"A referral is always the best client,
because somebody that they know, like and trust
is giving you an endorsement,
which gives them more confidence in you."

Bob:

There's nothing worse than wasting your time with a bad referral who takes up your energy and doesn't buy, or invests only at a low level. A book can be written to attract exactly the perfect customer you want to do business with, and repel the types that you don't want.

As we stated earlier, getting your book into the hands of potential clients is the best thing that you can do with it to get it working for you. If you give away a hundred copies of your book to potential perfect customers, there's no way that you won't regain your investment many times over.

The best place to get perfect customers is from your happy clients who are trying to refer you, but don't know what to say. You just can't rely on your clients to sell for you, and they don't really want to sell in the first place. While they love you and your business, they don't really know how to sell.

You can completely automate your referral system with a book. You simply have to give every one of your customers a book and ask them to pass it on. If you have a receptionist or staff, put them in charge of giving out your book to every customer. Your clients will love it—and, trust me, you will have some of them asking for stacks of your books. And you want to give them as many as they want.

When they start passing it out they get bragging rights. They'll say, "I know the author of this book, and I recommend them highly. By the way, when you do go in, let them know that you know me personally, and you'll get treated really well." People love passing out the book that way. It's just an automatic way to get referrals that know, like, and trust you.

A referral is always the best client, because somebody that they know, like and trust is giving you an endorsement and which gives them more confidence in you. On top of it, they get handed a book with insight into who you are, what you do, and the successes that you have. They come to you feeling that they already know you and are ready to buy.

If you start writing your book with the goal of using it to generate referrals, the investment you make in your book will pay you dividends for years. Books just aren't viewed as marketing. Brochures, fancy marketing materials, and multi-media packages are all seen as marketing, and they go in the garbage. But your book will sit on their desk or their bedside table, and they will make time to look at it. If they don't want it, they will think of someone to pass it on to, because that's what we do with books.

How often do your clients ask you, "Do you have any brochures or any materials that I can give to my friend?" This doesn't work very well, because brochures just aren't seen as very valuable and will get thrown out.

Business owners may have an information night or a talk that can explain their product or service, but even that may be too big a risk for somebody. It takes effort to come, and people are a little timid. They don't want to stick their necks out.

But giving a book to somebody is no risk, and it's high value. It allows the person to do their research on you and your business without feeling vulnerable.

Being the author of a book makes you look really good in their eyes. There are not a lot of people in society that are authors.

If you do speak or hold information nights, give your book to everyone in the audience. It doesn't even matter if you are a good speaker. Just the fact that you are an expert and an author at the front of the room elevates you in their eyes.

A lot of the times, if we speak at the Chamber of Commerce or just a general event of some type, there might be anywhere from twenty-five to one hundred people. We always make sure we have enough books for every person that hears us speak.

If you pass out your book to the right audience, it's just a given that you will get business. They might not even contact you or show up in your business the next day, week, or month. I've had people contact me as long as ten years later. They say, "Hi Bob. I have your book here that you gave me ten years ago. I'm ready to start." No one is ever going to hold onto a brochure that long.

When people ask for brochures, it's often because they haven't made up their mind about your product or service, and it's a nice way of ending the discussion. With a brochure, it's likely the last time you'll hear from them.

With a book, it's a different story. I know at least three people who have gotten calls from someone saying, "I read your book on the flight home, and you're exactly what I'm looking for."

The thing about other marketing materials is that they are costly. Getting a print ad, even a small one, for $400.00 is not going to do you a whole lot of good. Getting bigger ads—getting the back page ad or getting color—can cost you thousands of dollars. TV and radio ad prices are exorbitant, and you can easily run yourself into hundreds, if not thousands, of dollars a month on Facebook ads or Google AdWords. And all this advertising is only good for the time that you're actively paying to run it.

When you give away a book, it costs you $6.00 to $8.00. If you're thinking about giving away fifty books, you're talking $300.00 to $400.00. The book has legs. It will keep on working for you. If they don't read it, they won't throw it out. They'll either pass it on to somebody or drop it off somewhere, but it's not something that goes in the garbage.

It just continues to work for you. A print ad is good as the day it is printed or maybe a couple of days. Billboards are only good for as long as they're up. Bus ads are good when people see them drive by. And none of these media build any rapport or trust. But a book in their hands just keeps working for you. Give your clients as many books as they want, and encourage them to share them.

There are so many things you can do. You can have special giveaway times in your office or business. You can have holiday or Christmas mailers. Just get your existing clients to give you the name and address of friends they want to send a book to. Then, you mail a signed copy of the book to this person from the person that is referring them. You can even include a note from the person referring them. The person will feel like they are receiving a gift from a friend. It gets information about you into their hands from somebody that they know, like, and trust.

If you are at a tradeshow or event, have a stack of your books with you that you can hand out as your business card (on steroids). It will impress people. It will make them take a step back, really size you up, and see who you are. While all the other people were giving out business cards and they've already forgotten who they are, they will remember you, and they'll know what you're about or what you do.

The power of a book referral has been statistically proven to get clients or patients who spend more, stay longer, and refer like crazy. When you think about the compounding effect of a book, the lifetime value of your perfect customer will very likely go up.

Sometimes you see realtors put up a billboard for a month. A billboard can be as much as $2,000.00 a month. Well, some of them keep it up for twelve months. That's $24,000.00. But is there anything about seeing someone's face larger than life that makes you say, "I trust that person, and I think I'll call them"?

Invest that same $24,000.00 into marketing your business with a book, and your books will be your unpaid sales force out there in the field getting you clients twenty-four hours a day, seven days a week, three hundred sixty-five days a year.

They can even gain momentum as time goes on. Certain books, such as Think and Grow Rich, which was written in 1937, were powerful back then and are actually gaining momentum and relevance as time goes on. That's the type of book that we want to position ourselves with, as experts in our field. That book will continue to keep working for you day in and day out.

I have a friend—we didn't actually do his book but I wish we had, but it has been working for him for years. He mails out one hundred of his books each year to people he wants to do business with. Then he follows up with them. He does about $350,000.00 per year.

Me being the person I am, I love making money. I asked, "Why don't you just boost that up to 300 books so you have a seven-figure business?"

He said, "Listen, Bob. I've got the life of my dreams. All I do is send out those one hundred books and I can work part time and make my $350,000.00. I go on three really nice vacations a year with my wife and my kids. Why would I change a thing?"

As business people, we require clients to make an investment so we can stay in business. We're all in sales. However, for a lot of us, we're professionals or experts, but we never really got into our business because we like selling. We started our business because we needed to in order to help people with our expertise.

The beauty of using a book to generate referrals and to stimulate people to invest in our products or services is that it eliminates that desperate energy of pursuit. When we're needing clients, and we're chasing after them, it's never a pleasant energy. It's an energy of desperation.

When a lead receives a book, be it from an existing clients, you handing it to them, or them getting it in the mail, they are impressed by your author status. They become interested in you. They're thankful for receiving the book. They get to learn about you at no risk. They simply feel like they're receiving valuable information, and they see that you're associated with it. This creates the desire within them to want to ask you for help, so they end up pursuing you. They're the ones that want you.

The beauty of a book is its powerful simplicity. Simply by using the giveaway process mentioned in this chapter—mailing it to people, handing it out at events or networking, or giving it to clients to generate referrals—you will generate more business than you need. Your book is your unpaid sales force.

You write and publish the book—the right book—once. The book keeps working for you twenty-four hours a day, seven days a week, three hundred and sixty-five days a year. It never goes on vacation, never smashes up the company car, never asks for a raise—and, if done properly, it will actually keep upping your income each year.

There's no other type of positioning or way of marketing yourself that we know of that will provide you as much leverage as a book does. It gains momentum over time. It doesn't have a shelf life like a business card or a brochure or a billboard or an ad on the back of a bus. It just keeps working for you over and over again for years to come.

So few people do this, because they think that it's a lot of work. Although it can be a lot of work, if you start with the right goal in mind (building your business rather than selling the book), it can be actually quite easy. We've helped hundreds of people do this, and we have shared the templates that we use to write our books with you, so you can do it, too. Make sure you get them at CelebrityExpertAuthor.com/Templates.

CHAPTER 7:
HOW A BOOK KEEPS YOUR MARKETING POWERFUL, SIMPLE & EFFECTIVE

"I have been at events where just one book given to the right person has turned into a six-figure contact over a couple of years."

"Writing an expert book and using it to market your business can be the only strategy that you need to grow a thriving business."

You have already learned how powerful and simple using a book to market your business is. The problem is that it's so simple that most people don't believe that it's all you need. Really. If you use your book to promote your business, you don't need to do any other marketing. Isn't that a relief to know?

It's the 80/20 rule all over again. Twenty percent of your clients will account for eighty percent of your gross income and eighty percent of your referrals. Don't you always find that the leads who respond to ads and special promotions tend to be the ones who are demanding, price sensitive, and looking for any opportunity to complain? They take up 80 percent of your time and effort, yet only account for 20 percent of your gross income. The reason a lot of business owners fail or throw in the towel is because of draining, low-quality leads that come in bulk.

Imagine your business operating with only the top-quality 20 percent, and all you had to do was give away your book and keep giving it away to get them. This is how easy it is. Even if your assistant or staff just gave your book away to every customer who came through the door, the right book will attract the high-end clients and repel the low-budget ones.

To keep your marketing straightforward and simple, you want to stick to something that you know works, that is elegant and produces really high-quality leads. The big problem a lot of people run into is they get caught up in the strategy of the week.

It really is a lot of the blind leading the blind. We see it all the time. We know that certain marketing trends aren't working very efficiently anymore, but there's still a lot of people putting a lot of hard work into them. They might be putting hours into something like social networking or creating videos because someone is saying that you have to do it to keep up with trends.

The bottom line is that most strategies really don't work anymore. When you look at the effort that you need to put in and compare it to the return, you see that you should really just stop wasting your time and money.

That's one of the reasons why we love the book. It's an old school means of establishing your credibility and authority that worked really well forty years ago, and it's still working today. In fact, with all the online, faceless, impersonal advertising that's all the rage, it's working even better today. It's just not one of those fad marketing trends that everyone jumps on, overuses, and ruins. And it won't be, because people think it's too hard to do.

Bob:

The Facebook Live feature was added in April 2016. I think it had been out for a few weeks when I did a talk and the event organizer used the feature to stream it. One hundred eighty people were watching me do a talk in downtown Vancouver from Facebook. That's because the feature was new.

Now, when I check the views on similar situations, there may be one or two people watching. Meanwhile, we see the same people are getting on Facebook Live and doing a monologue every day because I'm sure someone said that that's the way to get clients.

There's just such a huge learning curve to applying these strategies. They're a lot of work to set up. You have to get your website set up properly, you need your landing pages. You need all sorts of things that people are happy to charge you for to set up, but that in itself is expensive.

If you miss a single step in the process, it just won't work. Ultimately, if you do get it working, you're getting people from the Internet (via social media) who don't know you. They're just jumping at a deal. They're looking for something cheap and they're looking to test something without any risk. You end up with a whole bunch of draining, complaining, broke tire-kickers.

When you do marketing properly, using a very simple and elegant system that attracts high-quality leads, you find that it's much less effort for a far bigger return. The leads, the perfect customers, and the business are already there. Your existing perfect customers and the network of people around you contain all the money your business wants and needs. A book is a high-end lead attraction and referral system. In an untrusting world, the best lead is a referral.

Building trust and credibility is getting harder and harder, especially on the Internet. People are a lot more skeptical today than they were last year, and it's worsening by the month. Being aware of this in your marketing is important because it takes that much more work to get past this on the Internet.

Generally, people won't make a buying decision on the Internet unless they know your business. For this reason, any time you have marketing material online, always offer a free copy of your expert book. When somebody receives a book, it takes them by surprise. It reconnects to a more personal and slower-paced part of them.

For a long time, we've been saying that old school is the new school. In this day and age when everything is getting automated and impersonal, a book placed in your perfect customer's hands, is something tangible that creates connection. Books are such a trusted form of knowledge and information exchange, and they have been for centuries. It's something that has legs, and it's going to keep on working.

In marketing, as with anything, simplicity is a beautiful thing. By focusing on one simple, effective strategy, you can stay focused, tweak what is working, and keep improving your results. The rewards are great.

The simpler you keep it, the more focus that you can maintain on the things you are good at. Remember, it's the 20 percent of your efforts that produce 80 percent of your results and income. Focus on your best clients and where they hang out. Your book, as a high-end lead attraction system, can be all you need to do for marketing (as long as you give out enough copies).

Many times, I've given out fewer than ten copies at a small talk, with a phenomenal return. I've been at events where just one book given to the right person has turned into a six-figure contact over a couple of years. If you become really consistent in always passing out copies of your book, that book will always be working for you. It's impossible not to get quality clients this way, and it doesn't take a whole lot of work.

All the marketing strategies out there, including the strategy of the week, are based on volume. You have to reach out to a lot of people for them to work. If you don't reach enough people, you won't get very many leads. The reason a book keeps your marketing so easy is you only need to put it into the hands of a few very specific people, to get the clients you need. The best part is you're not sifting through a pile of useless leads, wasting valuable time and energy.

Giving out a book works the 80/20 rule to your advantage. You use 20 percent effort to reach the 20 percent of people that you enjoy serving. You'll never go wrong with focusing all your marketing efforts on books and giving out books to the right people. It's been shown many, many times that people that come through your book are going to spend three times more money, stay three times longer, and refer you ten times more often to more people who you just love having in your business. When you think about the compounding effect, it really is just a completely different ballgame.

When you look at the lifetime value of a perfect customer, the return is phenomenal, and you have invested little time, energy, or money. The $6.00 to $8.00 per book that you have printed turns into thousands, if not hundreds of thousands, of dollars. The time, energy, and money that you put into writing your expert book is the best investment you'll ever make. You just need to know who your ideal client is, write the right book for them, and put it in their hands.

Dr. Paul:

An expert book can be done with very little effort to you. It can be really as simple as having a conversation with a writer who knows how to position your business to your perfect customer. They ask you the right questions to find out what value you offer your clients, and then they write the book really quickly. It's what they do for a living, and they're good at it.

We've seen some people get their book written and published in fewer than three months this way. Once you get that done, it just keeps on working for you and you never have to do it again.

You can just use our CEA Right Book Template, which is available at CelebrityExpertAuthor.com/Template. It follows the same format that we used to write this book. Bob and I dictated the content and had the recording transcribed. I then edited the content to make it sound the way we wanted it to.

But you don't even need to do that. You can get a ghostwriter to turn the transcript into a readable manuscript that still has your voice. Some people, like myself, still want to have their hand in writing it, but many business owners just want to get their book attracting clients, making money, and simplifying their marketing as soon as possible. As an entrepreneur, if you really want to move your business forward, a book is not really a luxury; it is a necessity.

The stories in your book are so important. They will make or break your book as a marketing tool. You want your stories to be so enthralling to your perfect customers that they tell them to other people. When they parrot your story, they are selling for you without knowing. And this just keeps the simple elegance of this marketing strategy working for you while you do the things you love to do.

Storytelling is as old as time. People have been telling stories from the time that they could sit around a fire and paint on cave walls. Stories are a way of creating connections among humans. With the right stories in your book, your leads will come into your business pre-sold. Your book does the selling for you. We have also included our storytelling template so you can gather up your compelling stories that will connect with your perfect customers.

Even if you don't think you have very good stories—and we are sure that you are wrong about that—you can actually tell other people's stories. They don't have to be well-known or stories everyone knows. In fact, it's better if they are new to the reader. They simply have to spark interest and make the reader say, "I want that."

You still create great emotional connection by reporting on someone else's story. Think about it. Barbara Walters and Oprah Winfrey are two of the greatest interviewers on the planet. They tell other people's stories and have become much more famous than the people that they interview. If you're not far enough along in your business to have success stories, talk about and report on other people's success stories in your business niche.

Ultimately, if your marketing is complicated, you won't want to do it, it will break down, and you won't get leads. Marketing can be really simple, straightforward, and to the point. Your book can be the perfect bait that attracts exactly the kind of client that you want to draw in. You don't want to waste your time and energy using anything and everything to attract everybody, or you'll burn out.

Writing an expert book and using it to market your business can be the only strategy that you need to grow a thriving business. Most of us didn't get into business to do sales and marketing. Get your book to do it for you so you can focus on what you're really good at.

CHAPTER 8:

HOW YOUR BOOK TAKES CARE OF MARKETING & SELLING SO YOU CAN FORGET ABOUT IT & DO WHAT YOU'RE GOOD AT

"As long as you keep giving your book away. . .
you can stop marketing because your book is
doing it for you."

Let's face it: Most of us did not get into the business or the profession we're in to be marketing and sales professionals. In fact, we may feel a bit like used cars salesmen anytime we have to put on our sales and marketing hat. The experts that want to focus on customer service, doing excellent work, and letting the results speak for themselves end up wondering where all the business is.

Meanwhile, the guy down the street is out there marketing, and his business is going gangbusters even though you've heard from his customers that he isn't half as good as you and they don't get near as much service from him.

The fact remains that we know marketing and sales are necessary evils. Even though we don't like it, we still have to do it. If we don't get over this roadblock, we will struggle or even go out of business. Not liking it does not give you a "Get Out of Jail Free" card.

It doesn't have to be painful or hard. We think you should do what you love doing. Just make sure what you need done is handled. That means the sales and marketing have to be taken care of, because if you don't do this, you're just out of luck.

Businesses don't survive without sales and marketing. In most cases, people tend to do a little bit of marketing. If they're lucky, they get busy for a while. Then, all of a sudden, they run out of customers. They panic and do a little more marketing, they're busy for a while, and then the cycle repeats itself. It's that "feast or famine" thing.

But if you put in a structure where your marketing's working for you all the time, you can break out of this cycle. You really want to make sure that you have a marketing system that works, because if you don't, your business will struggle.

If you're a professional, you likely got into business because you had to in order to put your skills to work. When I graduated as a chiropractor, I opened up shop. I ended up in business without even thinking about what that meant.

I found out quickly that people don't just come to you because your doors are open. I had to do something to generate business. To my horror, I had to ask people for money.

At first, I would have a little influx of customers and sales, and be making some money. I'd get comfortable focusing on the part I loved (working with my patients) and I wouldn't look up until things got tight and I had to pay bills. I'd try to think of the last thing that I did that got me a bunch of new patients. Then I'd run out and do it, hoping it would work again.

It's just no fun when we cringe at the thought of being marketers, and it's hard to make good money when we feel really slimy every time we have to go into sales mode. We just wish that someone else could take care of that part so we could just do what we're good at and what we enjoy doing.

Maybe we look for just that, but there are so many people out there who will sell you different marketing systems. It can be such a slippery fish. You just don't know which marketing strategy to choose, and it can be really expensive. They're all ready to line up and sell you these lead-generating systems, but all leads are not created equal. It doesn't take long to find out that the leads aren't what you think they are, and it just doesn't bring in the business that you thought it should.

It's really hard to hire someone to do your marketing or to pass it off. While many business owners are thinking, "I just want to do what I'm good at, and have somebody else take care of getting me clients," it's a wish that can't come true.

When you get somebody else taking care of your marketing, they're just thinking, "I just need to get bodies in the door." They think they know enough about what you offer to get the people that you want, but it never seems to work out. All the leads you tend to get seem to be tire-kickers. They're not really that interested. They bit at a really good special offer, and they want something free. They're not looking for the best level of service, the longest term of service, or the type of results that you want to give.

There's no one who knows the customers you like best better than you do. You know who your best clients are and you know what they're like. You know what they have to do or buy to get the results. You want leads that turn into these perfect customers who stay clients and make the investment that gets them good results. You want your business to be full of these perfect customers.

No one can explain what you do better than you can. You know how to tell your clients what you do. You know how long they need to be involved with your business, your products, or your professional services to get the results that you know you can get. It's really important that you have a hand in the marketing.

There really is no better way to get all this across to your potential clients than to have it all detailed in your expert book. It saves you from having to say the same things over and over again. All you have to do is get your book into the hands of people who can really use the benefits your business offers. If your book connects with them and speaks to the problems they have, they will turn into customers.

People have such short attention spans today that you only have a few seconds to get their attention. Most people aren't going to sit there and listen to you for more than a minute or two while you're explaining exactly how good your services are, but when you get the book in their hands, it gives you all the time in the world. People will take your book and sit down with it. They will go through it, look over all the chapters, and read the front and the back. It's like getting a half-hour meeting with them to explain exactly what you do, and they actually listen to you.

When your perfect customer takes the time to go through your expert book, it's as if you're telling them exactly how your products and services will help them without having to be there. Because a book is not seen as marketing, even if they don't read right through it, it's hard for them not to read the important parts (such as the front cover, back cover, and table of contents). When you do your expert book properly, these critical parts of your book will hook them into wanting to read more. Or, better still, it makes them want to call you before they even put the book down.

Because a book piques their interest, you get some of their most valuable and guarded assets: their time and attention. Your book tells them how you can help get the results they want, and they think it's great because they are reading about a solution to their problems. They don't think that you are marketing to them because they are impressed by the helpful information in your book. Your book gets them sold on turning to you for help with their problem, because now they know you're the expert. People love buying; they just don't like being sold.

When people are shopping, they're really suspicious of salespeople. When we walk into a store and a salesperson approaches us, we often tense up. That's exactly what we don't want happening when we're making our sales presentation. A book gets around that close-mindedness before they get to you.

People buy emotionally, but then they justify it with logic. The last thing you want to be doing when you are talking to them is battling it out with their logic. You want to connect with them in a fully emotional state so they say yes to the results you can get for them. Your book already gave them a chance to think through all the pros and cons and to connect with the success stories. They want to buy, but they want to make the decision. They want to be in control. When they reach you through your book, all this has already taken place. They want to drop some cash.

This is why it is so important to have great success stories throughout your book. You want to tell them about your products and services, and how they work to get the results your business provides. The more you use story, the better your book will market and sell for you. Not only will the story resonate with your perfect clients, you'll actually find that your perfect clients will start telling the story to others. They become your own personal salesperson without them actually knowing it.

When people have heard or read stories about you, they start to feel like they know you. They've gotten some insight into who you are, and you become less of a stranger to them. In fact, you may not know who they are, but they will come in and say, "Oh, I know all about you. I especially love that story about the woman you helped."

When they feel that kind of connection with you, you stop being a stranger and they are ready to buy. The key to handing off your sales and marketing is to do it with your book. You can let your book do all the work building the relationship, and all you have to do is keep the relationship going with them.

The only time that people will buy from strangers is when they think they're getting a real heck of a deal. That's exactly the type of clients that we don't want. We want people that are hiring us for our expertise because of the fact that we're the authority in our particular niche, and because we're the author of the book on the subject. We don't want people calling us just because they want the deal of the century.

Bob:

In my neighborhood a few years ago, these guys were driving around in white vans and approaching strangers. They'd say, "Do you want to buy a $1,000.00 pair of speakers for $100.00?"

Automatically, they would start thinking, "Wow, a $1,000.00 pair speakers for $100.00."

The guy would tell you the story why: "It's a shipment that fell off the back of the truck. They're not damaged, it's just the packaging that's damaged, but you're going to save $900.00."

A lot of people fell for that story, and they would tell others the story of the great deal they got. But the truth of the matter is they got $50.00 speakers for $100.00.

You don't want to ever get caught in that particular situation. When you position yourself with a book, you avoid that totally.

You can charge higher prices than everybody else once you have a book, because you're actually building the relationship based on credibility and expertise. There's no need to justify your prices, because people are seeing that your results speak for themselves. They're relating to stories about people just like them getting results that they want. Before you even open your mouth, they already see your value.

No more having to go out and hustle it to get customers, clients, or patients. You're not getting surges of leads that make you crazy, only to yield a handful of decent customers. The fear of things drying up and your business going back into famine mode is gone forever. You can have the confidence that the money will not dry up and, will actually continue to increase.

As long as you keep giving your book away, sending it to all your inquiries and sources that you want to connect with, and keep passing it out to your existing clients to generate referrals, you can stop worrying about marketing because your book is doing it for you.

And you can completely automate this. If you are paying someone to network or attend events for you, you just need them to hand out your book. If you have a receptionist, a secretary, or staff, just have them hand it out to every client or patient who comes through the door. You can have them mail the book to potential clients, leads, and people in your industry, and it will keep working for you.

You can't not get business if you do this. I'm a great believer in it, and I'm never proven wrong on this particular belief. If you have the right book and you hand it out to one hundred people that are potential clients, it is literally impossible to not get some business and, within a year, get quite a bit of business.

And it just keeps on working. We have clients who are still getting new clients from a book that they passed out ten years ago. As a matter of fact, one colleague of ours wrote his book in 1981, and he's still using it to get clients today. That's just amazing. There's no other marketing or sales tool that has that set of legs. A billboard, magazine, TV commercial, or radio commercial: they are all over the day that you stop paying. Not so with a book. And not only do you not pay for the advertising, people even pay to buy your advertising.

Now, we always recommend that you give your books away, but books have a perceived value. So most people will get it for free, but they'll still perceive it as a $10.00 or $20.00 book. They see that as getting value even though it's your advertising. But many organizations and associations where your perfect clients hang out see that value as worth paying for. Often, when you offer to speak to these organizations and associations and your book is relevant to their members, who are your perfect customers, they will pay for at least part, if not all, of the cost of your books.

Once you position yourself with your book as the expert in your particular niche, getting speaking gigs is really quite easy. As a matter of fact, I've never actually even had to ask for any of the speaking jobs that I've done. People have always offered them to me because I've given them a copy of my book. And whether it's twenty-five or two hundred fifty people, I always make sure that everybody in that audience gets a free book.

If the event planner is covering the costs of giving out your book, that's a bonus. But even if you're giving out your book at your cost to a room full of your perfect customers, you will get your return on investment in a big way. This approach has rewarded me handsomely for years, and it is still our preferred strategy for getting our best clients.

You don't need to worry about being a slick salesman, because people want to associate themselves with you. They buy into your products or services because they want to associate you, and if you have done a good job of describing what you offer in your book and the benefits of different levels of investment, they will even upsell themselves.

Start writing your book with the right goal in mind so that it takes care of the sales and marketing and you can just forget about it. Write it to suit the needs of your perfect customers. Position yourself as the expert in your niche, and you'll be writing the right book. You just have to do it once and you'll never have to sell again.

You will feel so confident and so proud to be handing that out as your business card that people will feel it. It's something that creates a real resonance and attraction, and it will be getting you clients and customers forever. They will stay longer, they will spend more money, and they will refer you more often.

Now that we've told you how a book does your sales and marketing for you, we want to take it up a notch and show you how you can use it to put your sales and marketing into overdrive. In next chapter, we'll be talking about ten ways to make more money in your business with your book.

Some of the methods may resonate with you, and some may not. The beauty of it is you only need to use one or two strategies with your book consistently, and you will always have more than enough business.

CHAPTER 9:
TEN WAYS TO MAKE BIG MONEY WITH YOUR BOOK

*"When you have the right book,
it is literally impossible to not get a return on your
investment many times over."*

If you use your book and do exactly what we've written in the previous chapters, you will already be attracting great clients, growing your business, and increasing your bottom line.

This chapter shares some great ways to leverage your book even more as a tool to build a thriving business. We know these strategies work because of the results we've seen with our clients, and the results that we've gotten in our own business.

You don't have to do them all. Simply pick one or two strategies that you resonate with, and make them a consistent habit. If you do this, you can trust that your marketing is handled and then forget about it. So let's get right into it.

#1. Use Your Book as a Business Card on Steroids

Bob:

I haven't had a business card for close to ten years. I've always passed out my book. When people ask for my business card, I purposely tell them, "I don't have a business card, but here's my book."

Of course, the nice thing about that is they never throw out my book which means that after they've thrown out everyone else's card, they are still holding onto my business card on steroids. It just solidifies the fact that you are the expert in that particular niche. They remember you, because there are very, very few people who you're going to hand your book to who have written a book, but they want to write one.

When you give someone a business card, that's like standard practice. When you give a book to someone that you just met, you get a reaction. You make an impression, and they're grateful for the gift. It's a really great way to stand out, and it's a way to make sure that you are remembered.

#2. Mail a Copy of Your Book to One Hundred Key Players in Your Industry

When you're writing your book or waiting for it to be published, sit down and create a list of one hundred people in your industry who you want to connect with. Think of the people who could bring you business if they knew more about the benefits that you provide. You may know who they are, you may have some connection with them, or you may not know them at all, but when you mail these books to them, it has a big impact.

I already mentioned my friend who uses this particular strategy. Every January, he mails out one hundred books to what he feels are perfect customers who he wants to work with. His follow-up throughout the rest of the year nets him $350,000.00 in part-time work. He spends the rest of the time enjoying life with his wife and two kids instead of worrying about where his next client will come from.

There is no limit to how much money you can make just by mailing out your book and getting into the habit of sending out a book to anyone who you connect with. Before you talk to someone, make sure they have received a copy of your book and have had a chance to go through it. If somebody's made an inquiry, get that book out to them as quickly as you can and follow up after that. Your meeting with them will make such a better impression, and whatever the results you are looking for will be highly likely to occur.

#3. Give Away Your Book at Any Event or Meeting You Attend

This is a strategy that is very effective because most experts, business owners and professionals go to meetings and events or associations of some kind, such as networking breakfasts. Maybe it's the Business Network International (BNI) or the local Chamber of Commerce. Sometimes we get invited to events, health fairs, or trade shows where maybe you're a sponsor. You might even have a booth or a table.

Have books available for everybody who comes by. If you're at a breakfast meeting, get a book placed at every seat before the meeting. That leaves a big impression. The event organizer will appreciate it and plug you to all the attendees, and everyone will be leaving with your business card on steroids.

Remember that this is not an expense that you should be looking to recoup through selling the book. This is some of the cheapest marketing that you can ever get. Every lead that could turn into a perfect customer probably has a lifetime client value in the hundreds of thousands of dollars.

#4. Be the Expert Speaker at Association Meetings & Put Your Book in the Hands of Key Players

This can be any type of meeting where there are people who are looking for solutions that you can provide. It could also be gatherings of people that could refer others to you. It doesn't have to be a big event, and you can even host these events yourself. Being the speaker and having your book in the hands of everybody in the room is such an effective way to generate business.

Many of our clients use this particular strategy of handing out their book to the entire audience for free. It's always worth checking to see if the event organizer is willing to pay for all or part of the cost of the books. At the end of the day, whoever pays for the books is inconsequential to you, because you're speaking to an audience of your perfect customers and you will get business.

#5. Hold New Client Information Sessions & Give Your Book Away to Generate High-Paying Leads

Dr. Paul:

This is something that I always did during my sixteen-plus years of practice because it attracted leads and brought in the best patients. I held these sessions anywhere from weekly to monthly. At that time, I didn't have a book, but I know for a fact that with the results I'm getting now, my conversions at those information sessions would have doubled if I had a book to give to each person.

When they attend these information sessions, they're still skeptical. They're expecting to be sold and you need to build trust. When you're speaking and you have your book, you have two things working in your favor to create authority, expert status, and trust.

#6. Give Away a Free PDF Version with Your Online Marketing, Social Media, or Facebook Ads

Bob:

It is now very popular to use social media and online marketing to get people to come into your business. The trick is that you have to get them offline and into your business. Use your book (you can mail a copy) or the free PDF as something to attract people. It gives them a chance to check you out, and it makes you stand out from the flood of online competitors.

Our client, Lisa Sasevich (LisaSasevich.com), author of The Live Sassy Formula, uses this strategy to generate tens of thousands of leads on Facebook. She is an expert in the area of creating sales from speaking, and has mentored Bob and me in that area. Using two very short, 50-page books and a massive Facebook campaign, she grew her mailing list by 70,000.

The book is something of value and it's low risk. They can opt in to get your book and read all about you. They're not really sticking their necks out, you get to build trust, and they sell themselves.

#7. Use a Free Book Giveaway to Attract Leads to Workshops, Dinner Events, and/or Webinars

Dr. Paul:

This is a good strategy to take people from online to offline. You can invite people on your mailing list to a free workshop or event and entice them even more with a free copy of your book. Lots of experts and professionals use events and workshops to attract perfect clients. Dinner events have been very effective for financial planners and chiropractors in attracting new clients.

Dr. John Peters (PacificClearMindCenter.com) has had great success from holding dinner talks to build his chiropractic practice. He often gets twenty people out to his event and will convert close to 100 percent of the viable leads to the next step of having a brain map done in his office. This often results in twelve new patients during the following week.

His forthcoming book about how brain maps help him to treat neuro-degenerative conditions like Alzheimer's, Parkinson's, and dementia, which will have a massive impact on the long-term results from his dinner talks.

We can't wait to see how being a published author and specialist increases the longevity of those new patients. A private workshop or dinner with the author of a book is a huge credibility builder.

#8. Use Your Celebrity Expert Author Status to Charge Higher Fees Than Your Competition

This is the most effective thing any expert, professional, or business owner can do to substantially increase their income. When we offer products and services that are comparable to our competitors, we have to deal with people shopping around for the best price.

If you buy into the price war, you become a commodity, which will drive your business into the ground. Live by price, die by price. You can only cut your price so much before life starts to become unpleasant.

But on the upside, when you're well-positioned with an expert book, there is literally no ceiling to what you can charge. When an expert identifies a system they use and names it as their specialized system, it becomes something that only they do. It doesn't matter if it's actually the same process that every other person in the industry uses. People see you as having a significant level of expertise that nobody else has.

Candace Plattor, a family addiction recovery therapist, has used this strategy to sell $20,000.00 family programs rather than competing with her peers who charge $100.00 per hour.

#9. Get Featured as a New Author in Newspapers & Magazines

This is something that's actually quite easy to do, because local newspapers and magazines are always looking for stories. They're usually at a shortage and are looking for things to write about. Authors are always a hot and interesting topic.

Mail your book or hand it to the reporter, and they will more than likely just jump at the opportunity to do a story on you and talk about your book. Be clear that you are offering the readers a free copy of your book, and be sure to include a way for people to get their hands on it, whether it's via a link to your website or just your phone number.

Newspapers and magazines can be very sensitive to the idea of an entrepreneur trying to get free advertising. They are even skeptical of press releases. But when someone who is an expert in a particular area has a new book, that's newsworthy.

#10. Capitalize on Your Author Status to Get a Spot on Local Television

Local television stations are also looking for stories to run, and they love authors. Simply contact the TV station in your area. Tell them you're an expert in your niche and that you have a new book. They will be happy to interview you.

This gets you even more reach. The number of people that are actually watching these shows is surprising. Again, just make sure that you have a way to get your book into the hands of the viewers.

Being an author and expert on TV adds another level of credibility to you, and you can put the clip on your website and use it to build your celebrity status. Quite often, if you provide valuable insights, you will be asked back even several times a year. You can even be asked to be their resident expert.

****

These are ten strategies that we have seen work effectively with our clients and in our own business to generate high-end leads, get really great clients and increase our bottom line.

When you have the right book, it is literally impossible to not get a return on your investment many times over. In fact, it actually takes effort to make an expert book fail. However, if you were hell-bent on not getting results, here are the things to do.

#1. Be a Perfectionist

This will absolutely paralyze you. We have seen everything from people who are trying to write the perfect book and never get it done, to people who won't hand their book out because it has a typo. People will always criticize you, and you can't protect yourself. The best way around them is to make a lot of money.

#2. Worry about What Your Peers Will Think

A lot of experts, especially professionals, have this issue. They don't want to say something because they're afraid of criticism from their peers. Being an author just takes stepping past the fear and doing it anyway.

#3. Wait to Take Action

Many people are waiting until they have a certain qualification, until they learn or master something, or until their website or branding is set up to take action. They never take the action and they never get it done. Start before you think you're ready, and you will be amazed by the results.

#4. Complicate Things

This doesn't have to be complicated. All it takes is writing your book, saying what you need to say, and not worrying about it. Get it done so your book can start working for you. Go with imperfect action and "good enough," because you are taking a step that few people ever take.

#5. Get Discouraged & Put Your Book Up on the Shelf

Sometimes, people hand out a couple of books and don't get the response they want. Or someone points out a spelling mistake or grammatical error early on. It's unfortunate if that happens on the first couple that you hand out, but the odds are totally with you. If you hand out one hundred books to your perfect customers, it will be impossible to not get a return.

It's only a matter of time. Once you start getting results, success breeds success and you'll want to hand out more. Don't let the little things stop you. We have seen too many people put a perfectly good book up on the shelf. When we find out about it, we tell them, "Grab that book off the shelf and get out there."

Susan Swim (SusanDelanoSwim.com) is a seven-figure entrepreneur and business coach. She and her husband own a very successful window cleaning company. It does so well because Susan has a formula for creating high-performance teams in the usually transient manual labor industry.

She told us of an opportunity she had to speak to forty women. When we asked her if she planned get any business out of it, she said no; she was just going to inspire them to live their best life.

Susan had co-authored a book called Answering the Call with her mentor, Lisa Sasevich, but she did not like how the book turned out and had boxes of them in her closet. We told her to bring a copy for every lady in the audience and invite them for a complimentary discovery coaching session with her.

The next time we spoke, she told us that twenty-seven of the forty women had signed up.

The only thing that will keep your book from working for you are your messed up thoughts. Putting yourself and your opinions out there makes your mind go crazy, and then your mind just says, "Who am I to write a book about this? What will my peers say?"

Get over yourself and stay focused on the right goals. You want to make money in your business and you want your book working for you, getting your perfect customers.

CHAPTER 10:
GETTING IT DONE: THE SIMPLE PATH TO AUTHOR & BUSINESS SUCCESS

"The book is already in you. It's part of who you are, and it's waiting to come out. The sooner you do it, the sooner you can claim its value and get it working for you."

"Fear is what's keeping us from our greatness. Action is the antidote to fear."

An idea is worthless without action. How long have you wanted to write a book? How long has it been in the idea phase? Can you even calculate how many opportunities and how much money has passed you by because you did not take action and write your book?

Having a book that does your sales and marketing for you is only a nice idea until you write the book. It's time to put all your excuses and justifications for why it's not done to rest for good. Writing and publishing a book is much easier than you think. The content of your book is already inside you and is just waiting to come out.

When you start your book with the right goal and create a clear path to your desired outcome, success is inevitable. Our expert book-writing process and the CEA Right Book Template make this a no-brainer. Download your copy at CelebrityExpertAuthor.com/Templates. This is the exact template we used to write this book and many, many other successful experts' books.

The first thing to remember is you're not writing a Pulitzer Prize-winning book. We can't stress enough that imperfect action is better than procrastination and perfectionism. This is one of the biggest obstacles that paralyzes most people when they want to write a book or take a step towards their real dreams and goals. It holds us in fear and doubt, and it keeps us from ever achieving anything that we want.

Bob:

A "good enough" book that you run with will always outperform the perfect book idea that never gets written. Start that book. Get it written. Get it done fast, and you can start enjoying the benefits of using a book for your sales and marketing. You'd never have to worry about marketing again.

All this is only commentary if you don't have your book done. We can explain it all we want, but unless we actually have our book that we can pass to our perfect customer, it's all talk. We're wasting our time even writing about it. Just get it behind you, put in that effort once, and reap the rewards of it.

So many people use the "I'm working on my book" excuse. It's really more of a justification that keeps you from feeling bad about what you're not doing.

I've been teaching a class for almost ten years now on how to write and publish your book in forty days. I've taught thousands of people over the years.

I met a lady in one class who has actually been writing her book since 1968. I asked her, "Why don't just finish it and get it working for you?"

By the end of the class, she said she was completely motivated to get her book done. But then she went back to her writers group and fell back into her "I'm working on it" pattern. Last time I checked, she was still working on it.

Dr. Paul:

You can get this done fast. Ninety days is a reasonable amount of time to budget for getting your book done, and that does not involve taking time away from your business. Some people will do it even faster than that. I actually had one lady get her book written and published in twenty-eight days. Most people get their expert book written and published in around six months, but ninety days is very doable.

When we help people write their book, we simply guide them in filling out the CEA Right Book Template. The first page is the most crucial because it is all about positioning your products and services to your perfect customer. You want to be very clear about the pains that this person has and the results that they are looking for. This section will help you to clearly articulate how you solve your perfect customer's problem in your business.

You want to use this information to come up with your transformation. Your transformation tells the perfect customer exactly what they can expect to gain from reading your book and, ultimately, from doing business with you. Our transformation is: You can automate the attraction of perfect customers and never have to do sales and marketing again when you write and publish an expert book and use it to grow your business.

We like to capture an expert's passion, so we always have them share their ten biggest successes with us. We then use the storytelling template, which we provided for you to download, to tell the story in a way that is compelling to the perfect customer. People will forget everything you say but they will remember how you made them feel. Stories convey a feeling and people will remember your stories. You will want to use these stories to support or even convey the information in your ten chapters.

We then decide on ten topics that your perfect customers need to know about their problem, the solution, and how your business delivers this solution. We simply write a list of topics and see which ones are the most relevant. These topics become each of the chapters in the template. To make them a good chapter title, we turn each topic into a headline that makes the perfect customer want to read the chapter.

Once we have decided on the chapters, we break each chapter into about five key points that you will discuss. This creates a nice framework for your book and gets you set up so you can start writing on any one of the topics that you have broken your chapters into. You don't have to start in order, and if you get writer's block on one topic, simply move on to another.

By filling out the CEA Right Book Template, you are breaking up your subject matter into easy-to-write-about chunks that you can work on in 45-minute blocks. You just need to carve a 45- to 60-minute block out of your day.

When you have all your information laid out in a logical manner and you have it chunked into sections that you can easily explain, writing the book is not such a big job. Instead of starting at the beginning and tackling the whole book, you can simply focus on one chunk at a time. This way, you don't go off on tangents and you don't get writer's block. It's not hard when all you have to do is focus on one topic and write all you know about it.

Your goal is to write a 120-page book. That's really the sweet spot, because it's enough pages that people consider it a book, but it's short enough that it doesn't cost much to print. It doesn't weigh a lot, so it's easy to carry a bunch of them your briefcase or in your suitcase, and it doesn't overwhelm people when they get it.

A book this size is about 30,000 words. When you break it down into ten chapters, each chapter is about 3,000 words. Each chapter is broken into five key points, which is 600 words per key point. You have a total of fifty points to write about. You can do this over fifty consecutive days—or let's just say two months. The total writing time is only thirty-seven and a half to fifty hours.

The book's already in you. It's part of who you are, and it's really waiting to come out. The sooner you do it, the sooner you can claim its value and get it working for you.

There are some fast-track options. If writing your book in fifty days isn't fast enough, you can dictate your book, especially if writing isn't your thing. Instead of writing about one of your fifty points, speak about it and record it.

You can use the interview process, which means that you can have somebody ask you questions about the points in your template. You may want to break each point down further into sub-points to help with this process.

In fact, that's how this book has been put together. Bob and I just had a conversation about each chapter, and we completed the recording for one to two chapters each day. We had completed the entire content in a week.

Lots of people come to us when they are at a standstill with their book. We just help them tweak their template, and then we assist them in a number of different ways, depending on how much work they want to do themselves. If you just want your book done with the least effort possible, the option to go with is the ghostwriter. This person can take your template, interview you, and then write the manuscript from start to finish in your voice.

If you still want to do the writing yourself but you don't want to start with a blank page, we can interview you and provide you with a transcript to work from. That is what I did to write this book. I had the recordings from Bob's and my conversations transcribed, and then I edited the transcripts. The transcripts come back verbatim, so every 'so', 'you know,' and any other strange ways you speak show up. These need to be turned into a more written style, while maintaining the conversational nature and your voice.

When you get the manuscript to your liking, you need to have it edited for grammar and spelling. You may actually want to get a more structural edit, and you can hire people to do this. I don't mind doing that myself for my own books, but we have people on our team who are very good at this.

There are four people who can save you hundreds of hours of procrastination and wracking your brain when it comes to getting your book done fast. I've already mentioned them, but I'll list them here:

1. The interviewer asks you questions about your template and records what you say.

2. The transcriber takes the recording and produces a word-for-word transcript that you can work from.

3. The ghostwriter turns your transcript into a readable manuscript that still maintains your voice.

4. The editor goes through your manuscript for spelling, grammar, consistency, and flow.

You may fulfill the role of all four people yourself, or perhaps you will get help from one or more of these people. We have been working with a team of these people for years to assist our experts in getting their books done quickly.

Bob:

Remember, it doesn't have to be perfect. I've had one of my books out for ten years, and someone actually wrote to me to point out all the mistakes in my book. There were just pages of them, in her opinion. I thanked her very much and let her know that I would consider all her changes in the second edition.

The funny thing is, this lady does not have a book and is not making any money from a book, but she pointed out all the problems with mine. Granted, my book had some mistakes I wanted to fix (not nearly as many as she thought I should), but it's been generating multiple six-figures in business for years.

So don't let the fact that your book isn't perfect stop you from moving forward. Some of the top books in the world, such as those by Deepak Chopra or Wayne Dyer, have a mistake or two in them.

Don't let any of this crap get in your way. Your book is inside you. You already know all the information and you already have something to say. There's not a whole lot of research to do first. Just start writing it; it wants to come out. Fear is what's keeping us from our greatness. Action is the antidote to fear.

You don't need any more information. In fact, you need less. In 120 pages, you must make your points concisely. You want to get exactly the right information across to the people who you want to move to action, so ask yourself, "Is what I'm waiting for to get started just an excuse or an alibi?"

Whenever you think you need to provide more information and more facts, remember that people don't want to read this. It's not interesting to them, and it doesn't help them.

The real stories about real people who have gotten great results with your work, your products, or your services make a big difference for them. You can always explain something by using an example or a story.

Most people can't really tell a story properly to make it interesting, but with a little tweaking, you can make a really boring story into a killer story. Our storytelling template guides you in making your success stories interesting and compelling. If you're the new kid on the block and you don't have your own success stories, you can be the reporter on someone else's story.

There's a story out there that I've heard so many people use in their talks or tell in their books. It's been told many, many times over. The story was about a study that was done with the Harvard class of 1979. They asked the graduates, "Have you set clear, written goals on your future and made plans to accomplish them?" Three percent had written goals and plans. Thirteen percent had goals that were not written. The final 84 percent had no specific goals at all.

When they followed up ten years later to find out where these graduates had ended up, the 13 percent who had goals but had not written them were earning, on average, twice as much as the 84 percent of those who had no goals at all. The 3 percent who had clear, written goals were earning, on average, ten times as much as the other 97 percent of graduates all together.

But here's the thing. This story's been told for literally decades now, and it's not even true. Harvard has gone back and tried to authenticate this story. It did not happen, but it's a powerful story. You'll probably remember the story, but it's not my story, and it's not true.

Now, you want to make sure that your stories are true, because you want to stand behind them. We can't emphasize the power of a story enough. It makes the difference between a book that converts leads into clients and a book that sits on the shelf gathering dust.

Some of the stories in our book were brought up more than once to make a point. One story can often prove several points. Making a point does take repetition, so you will want to have a fair bit of repetition in your book. It's actually mandatory. So if you find that your content is repetitive, that's okay. The biggest authors in the success industry today emphasize the importance of repetition in their personal development and self-help books.

It makes us feel good because we feel that we're understanding things. If your book is too full of information, it will be boring and difficult to follow. If your book is the "how to" guide, people will think they can do it all themselves, and then they will do nothing. If, however, your book just makes sense to them and the process seems so simple and obvious, they will come to you for the results.

There is nothing else to do but get started. Once you put in the work, you'll never have to do it again. The perfect book that never gets written will do nothing for your business at all. The "good enough" book that you run with will keep paying you for years. You'll be able to focus your passion into what you love and watch your business and dreams expand. What's it going to be? Are you ready?

CONCLUSION

It is so important to write the right book if you want to have it handle your sales and marketing on autopilot while you focus on what you love about your business. That's why we have provided the CEA Right Book Template and the CEA Storytelling Template. CelebrityExpertAuthor.com/Templates If you complete these templates before you start your book, you will be on the right track.

A lot of business owners are so caught up in the products and services they provide that they have trouble seeing their value through the eyes of their perfect customer. That's why a little guidance with the targeting of their templates can be extremely valuable in making sure they write the right book.

Most of the time, when someone comes to us for publishing and their book is already written, it is the wrong book. We will gladly format it, put a nice cover on it, and upload it into distribution, but sadly, it will not have the desired effect of automating their sales and marketing. It really is a shame when authors come to us at that point because it is too late to do anything with the manuscript unless they want to start over. It is so costly if you start out on the wrong foot.

For those of you who want to make sure you are on the right track and get the right focus for filling out your CEA Templates, you will want to talk to Bob and me on a CEA "Write the Right Book" call.

This is a 90-minute session where you, Bob, and I will figure out how to make your book the most attractive it can be to your perfect customer. We will address the most important positioning aspects of the CEA Right Book Template so that your chapters and the stories in your CEA Storytelling Template connect emotionally with the perfect person that you want to fill your business with.

This is a service that we charge $497.00 to provide; however, if you use the code "RIGHTBOOK," you will get it for $97.00. You can purchase this on our website at www. CelebrityExpertAuthor.com/RightBook.

Every month, we give away five free CEA "Write the Right Book" calls. To see if you qualify, email Cindy, our administrative assistant (Cindy@CelebrityExpertAuthor. com) or call (866) 492-6623 and ask if we have any free spots left. If there is one available, Cindy will be happy to help you schedule the time with Bob and me.

We are excited that you are taking the next steps to becoming a published author, and we are here to assist you along the way. We know the impact on your life and business will be absolutely transformative.

We wish you great success with minimal effort,
Bob and Dr. Paul

ABOUT
CELEBRITY EXPERT AUTHOR

Celebrity Expert Author is a pay-to-publish niche publishing house where our passion is helping experts, business owners, and professionals write and publish an expert book.

We specialize in ensuring that people write the right book that positions them as the leading expert and specialist in their field. Our main focus is delivering a book that targets their perfect customer and shows them exactly why they should choose this expert over their competitors.

The end goal is a book that is really a powerful sales and marketing tool that is used to grow your business and profits.

Product & Service Offerings

1. Publishing & Distribution

We assist authors with publishing ready manuscripts by providing them with title and subtitle assistance, cover design, back cover copy and design, and book formatting. We publish the book and upload it to our distribution system, which makes their book available to 31,000 online and offline bookstores in Canada, the United States, the United Kingdom, and Australia.

2. Proofing & Editing

We provide this service when an author's manuscript is not publishing ready so that we may publish it and upload it to our distribution system.

3. "Writing the Right Book" Assistance

For people who want guidance to ensure that they write the right book to attract their perfect customers and grow their business, we provide a variety of options depending on how much assistance the need. These include:

- Guidance with the CEA Right Book Template and CEA Storytelling Template to create a complete structure, outline, and storyline for their book.

- Guidance and accountability in the writing process.

- Interviewing and transcription for authors who don't want to start their book with a blank page in front of them.

- Ghostwriting and editing for authors who are struggling with turning their spoken content into readable written content.

4. "Completely Done for You" Book

This is for busy professionals, business owners, and entrepreneurs who want the benefit of getting their expert book done fast, without the hassle of writing and taking time and focus away from their business.

We work with you from start to finish to ensure that your book targets your perfect customer. We complete the CEA Right Book Template and CEA Storytelling Template to create a complete structure, outline, and storyline for your book. Then we provide a ghostwriter to gather the necessary information and write the book in your voice.

This is the most efficient way to get an expert book finished. A ghostwriter only requires a few hours of interview time to get all the necessary information to produce the final manuscript.

We then assist with the title and subtitle and take care of cover design, back cover copy and design, and book formatting. Finally, we publish the book and upload it to our distribution system.

To take advantage of any of these services,
please email Cindy, our administrative assistant, at
Cindy@CelebrityExpertAuthor.com
or call (866) 492-6623.